SPARK IN THE STUBBLE

LESLIE CHARLTON

SPARK IN THE STUBBLE

Colin Morris of Zambia

In the time of their visitation,
they shall shine, and run to and
fro like sparks in the stubble.

WISDOM OF SOLOMON 3:7

LONDON
EPWORTH PRESS

© Leslie Charlton 1969
First published in 1969
by Epworth Press
(Book Steward
Frank H. Cumbers)
printed and bound by
C. Nicholls & Company Ltd

SBN 7162 0121 6

For Daphne,
to whom this book and
this author
are dedicated

FOREWORD

BY HIS EXCELLENCY DR. KENNETH KAUNDA

President of the Republic of Zambia

COLIN MORRIS is widely known throughout Central
Africa as the Fighting Parson. He is a rare combination of
brilliance, honesty and loyalty to Man. There is no doubt
in my mind that the Church as I know it needs the origi-
nality of his thought as well as the power of his oratory to
convey to that organization the realization that Man does
not live in watertight compartments of religion and politics.

During our troubled years, he rarely delivered a non-
political Christian message from his pulpit. He preached
with such courage and conviction that the Government of
the now-defunct Federation of Rhodesia and Nyasaland
were threatening to deport him every other week. By not
deporting him, of course, they denied him a hero's welcome-
back to Northern Rhodesia, now reborn as the Republic of
Zambia.

It is my firmly held belief that Man, in spite of his
immeasurable weaknesses and difficulties, is slowly moving
towards an ideal society. With its message of love I believe
the Church has an important rôle to play in bringing about
such a society but, of course, this depends in turn on how
well the Church receives the revolutionary message men
like Colin Morris are preaching. It is clear to me that Colin
Morris, like revolutionaries in other walks of life, was born
ahead of his time. For me, he is the ideal parson.

Recently he has added another book to his formidable
list of publications, but this time specifically on the work
of the Church. Again, the title of this book, *Include Me Out!*,
reveals the strong inner feelings which make a man fight,

5

work and think as he does. This book has, I understand, provoked angry comments from various quarters of the Church. It is a revolutionary work which, while at the moment it provokes anger, will, I am sure, be commonly accepted in a few decades from now.

The Fighting Parson is still fighting. Fortunately his battleground spreads far wider than the confines of the Church.

Kenneth David Kaunda

State House
Lusaka
Republic of Zambia

INTRODUCTION

WHAT follows does not pretend to be a biography of the
Reverend Colin Manley Morris. It is nothing more than a
lightning sketch of an extraordinary man who, in the
Central African countries of which for a time he was the
paramount Conscience, is loved and loathed with equal
passion.

His championing of the cause of Africans during the
years of the freedom struggle in the Federation of Rhodesia
and Nyasaland earned him such titles as 'Rhodesia's
Trevor Huddleston' and 'The Best Hated Man in Central
Africa'. He is credited with, or more often accused of,
having done more than any other individual apart from
Dr Kenneth Kaunda and Dr Hastings Banda to help
destroy the Central African Federation. Orders banning
him from South Africa, Rhodesia, and the Portuguese
territories are a back-handed tribute to the degree of
nuisance he became to white-minority Governments.

Unlike nationalist leaders Morris had no mass movement
behind him, striking and rioting to underline his demands.
His only weapon was a wooden object of furniture now
regarded as an antique in the modern world – a pulpit;
that, and a handful of dedicated Christians who supported
him through thick and thin and paid a heavy price for their
loyalty. It wasn't even a pulpit strategically placed in some
great cathedral or city church, but one standing in a tiny
building in a small, land-locked town in the interior of
Central Africa. From that remote spot, his voice rever-
berated to such effect throughout Africa and beyond that
every means from the desecration of his church, the public
burning of his books, threats of deportation, physical

violence, and an avalanche of abuse was used in attempts to silence him.

This is a story of the Church Militant at its most strident and violent. It is about the harm as well as the good that was done by a parson who refused to stay within the bounds of the ecclesiastically permissible, who tore up the rule book and put his foot through the stained-glass windows to let into his church the harsh light of an underprivileged world.

Above all this is the story of an incorrigible rebel who at thirty-nine is head of the largest Protestant Church in Zambia; a devout man whose language is ripe and whose behaviour so unclerical as to prompt the question: what is this man doing in the Ministry? Colin Morris, brilliant, moody, unpredictable, is the unlikeliest of crusaders whom God used to wage war on the forces of intolerance and cruelty that held back the peoples of Central Africa from inheriting their Promised Land.

I am a journalist, not a theologian. I first latched on to Colin Morris because he was 'news' and I found myself in the course of my job reporting his speeches. Sheer curiosity prompted me to probe deeper into the man behind the headlines for he seemed too 'impossible' to be true. I tell this story because I think it is an action-narrative well worth recording. Its theological significance I must leave to those qualified to assess it. Mine is the viewpoint of the man in the street, and, I would submit, a perfectly legitimate one; for if it requires a degree in theology to make sense of the witness and writings of prominent churchmen then there has been a serious failure of communication somewhere. Whether Colin Morris is orthodox or heretical I wouldn't know, but, as a journalist who worked for Zambia's national daily newspaper, I am in a position to know that his ideas helped change the face of a nation, and that alone makes them important.

Originally I regarded Morris with that weary cynicism Press men develop through having to sit, with notebook open, at the feet of public figures – an angle from which the

8

clay is often all too visible. He is now a firm personal friend who has viewed the writing of this book with a somewhat jaundiced eye, not because he fears criticism – he was hardened against that years ago – but because he refuses to believe that the story should be told. In fairness to him, I ought to quote from the letter he wrote in response to my original suggestion that I should write the book: 'I am dead against it. Biographies should be written about successes or failures. I have had my share of both, but am not yet either. I would not quarrel with an account of my Church's struggle in Zambia, provided the personal angle is played down. It was a co-operative venture and should be re-membered as such. . . .' I hope I have done justice to the loyal band of Christians who distinguished themselves in the freedom struggle, but the personality of Colin Morris overshadows the whole story, and in honesty that is the way I have told it.

Colin Morris's time in Africa is now drawing rapidly to a close. An exciting phase of his life is coming to an end, and I felt that some account of his African years should be set down whilst memories are still fresh and materials available. I hope what judgements the book contains are sober, but if they are tinged with admiration it is because a worthwhile job of work deserves a favourable report. There are enough 'insiders', both clerical and lay, busy 'knocking' the Church. Let an 'outsider' give credit where it is due. I challenge anyone reading this story with an open mind to dismiss the Church as irrelevant. When the crunch came in Central Africa, Christians were awake and fighting, and, for once, on the right side !

In the early chapters I have drawn heavily upon Colin Morris's own account of his first five years in Africa, *The Hour After Midnight*, published by Longmans Green in 1961 and now out of print. Maggie Senogles, Colin Morris's secretary, was a great help to me in writing the book once she overcame her initial and legitimate suspicion of my motives for writing it.

Lastly, and most important, I am honoured that His

Excellency, Dr K. D. Kaunda, President of the Republic of Zambia, a close friend of Colin Morris and a unique judge of the Church's effectiveness in the political struggle, consented to contribute the Foreword.

LESLIE CHARLTON

Chingola, Zambia
Independence Day, 1968

ACKNOWLEDGEMENTS

The author is grateful to the following for permission to quote from their publications: the Cargate Press (*Nothing to Defend*, Colin Morris); Clarendon Press (*Zambia, The Politics of Independence*, D. Mulford); Lutterworth Press (*Anything But This!* and *Out of Africa's Crucible*, Colin Morris); S.C.M. Press (*Christians of the Copperbelt*, Taylor and Lehmann); the United Society for Christian Literature (*Black Government*, Kenneth Kaunda).

I

'TAKE away the blue sky, and this could be Barnsley or Wigan or South Wales' wrote the twenty-six year old Colin Morris in his diary on the day in April, 1956, when he arrived in Chingola, Northern Rhodesia. He admits at that moment to a pang of disappointment that he would not endure the pioneering hardships he was anticipating with something like relish. As he inspected the unexpected comforts of his manse a copy of Trevor Huddleston's *Naught For Your Comfort* lay buried and forgotten in his half-unpacked luggage.

Until three days before, when he disembarked at Cape Town prior to the 2,000 mile rail journey north, Huddleston's book had been his lodestar. He was not the first missionary to pack it alongside his Bible. Huddleston's searing passion against racial discrimination had aptly confirmed for Morris a viewpoint on colonial Africa that he had absorbed in theory at Nuffield College, Oxford, from African specialists such as Dame Margery Perham, Kenneth Robinson, Ruth Schacter and David Apter.

Now he was no longer sure. His firmly-held beliefs and preconceptions had been blown to smithereens on first physical contact with the continent, an anti-climax experienced by probably nine out of ten newcomers feeling it beneath their feet for the first time. He felt disappointed, cheated.

His crusading spirit was jolted the moment he stepped ashore from the *Stirling Castle* clutching, as a pathetic gesture of defiance, Huddleston's book. It had crossed his mind that by possessing it he might be arrested on the spot, and if not straightway declared a prohibited immigrant at least thrown into the local jail. He was utterly convinced he was entering a police state, and he felt morally bound to establish from the start where he stood in the ideological conflict which runs through every seam of South African life.

He soon received his first shock. The uniformed official at the customs shed did not even glance at the book, let alone confiscate it. He simply took one look at Morris's clerical collar, gave him a hearty greeting in a thick Afrikaans accent, and waved him through. A baffled Morris made his way up Adderley Street, one of Cape Town's main thoroughfares, to kill time before the departure of his train. Huddleston's book was boldly displayed in virtually every bookshop window.

There was more in store. In the centre of another busy street, a coloured policeman stood on a dais directing the Master Race's traffic. There was no sign of non-Europeans slinking about their business as beasts of burden, cowed under the watchful eyes of European overlords armed with *sjamboks*. Morris watched two Africans jostle a European off the pavement as they larked about. According to the text book, this was the point at which a whistle should have shrilled and thug-like policemen materialized to march off the culprits for a thorough beating up. Instead the European stooped to dust off his trousers, muttered a few rude words, and went on his way with the laughter of the Africans following him down the street.

In the short space of an hour, all that Morris had come to believe about South Africa tumbled like a house of straw bricks. The foundations, too, became rubble when he saw Europeans and non-Europeans mingling indiscriminately on the upper decks of the trolley buses that ran through the city centre.

Today he knows enough about the mechanics of racial discrimination to avoid exaggerating the significance of incidents like these. But at the time he found them totally irreconcilable to all he had been led to believe. He was not the first to find himself in this disturbing position, nor will he be the last. Only the practical experience of living in Africa for a lengthy period can bring into correct focus, for instance, the strange gaiety with which South Africa's Coloured and African races contrive to live under *apartheid*, or 'separate development'.

As the Kaffir Mail roared across South Africa, Bechuanaland (now Botswana), on through Southern Rhodesia and the dense bush of the north, the moving picture of Africa which rushed past the window of Morris's stuffy compartment was a challenge from a different direction of all his prior assumptions. Many of the Africans he saw lounging about the numberless wayside stations at which the train called were undeniably filthy, and appeared childishly irresponsible. Nor were the sprawling *kraals* and corrugated iron shacks stretched out along the single track any compliment to the culture of the African peoples.

Morris's travelling companion was a Chisamba farmer who, uninvited, gave him a non-stop commentary on 'Life with the Kaffir'. He regaled him with amusing anecdotes about the behaviour of his African farm 'boys'. It was very impressive because the farmer spoke of his workers with a reluctant kind of affection, though without any illusions.

By the time the train came to a stop at Ndola – gateway to Northern Rhodesia's rich Copperbelt, and seventy miles from Chingola – Huddleston was already losing badly on points. Mentally Morris, in his own words, had begun to slide down the greasy pole of rationalization whose base was firmly embedded in the White Settler Point Of View.

At the time Morris took up residence, Chingola was the most northerly of the Copperbelt's network of six small towns, a self-contained miniature welfare state wholly dependent on the neighbouring Nchanga Copper Mine to which it owed its existence. As with the other copper towns, every amenity was available. Such amenties were, and still are, part and parcel of a social obligation undertaken by the mining companies since the 'twenties when the first ore was torn from the reddish earth and the first copper

13

wirebars cast. The Copperbelt itself, bejewelled with the gems of the mining towns, is, in tempo, reminiscent of the Yukon of old. An *Observer* correspondent described it as 'an African phantasy beside which Timbuktu and the Mountains of the Moon are trifling, mundane items'. It is an incredibly wealthy slice of land set down in the heart of thousands of square miles of the most desolate bush imaginable.

From Ndola, which doggedly maintains the aspect of a Wild West frontier town in spite of all the efforts of its sophisticated town planners, a broad tarmac highway cuts a black, polished swathe through the limitless forest of stunted trees, bisecting giant red clay ant hills. On and on it goes, paralleling the spidery steel pylons which convey the power by which the Copperbelt lives.

Speeding along this main road in the middle of nowhere, one is so hypnotized by the bars of light and shade caused by sun and trees which flick across one's sight, that it is a physical shock to breast a rise and see stretched out ahead the red and green roofed villas of a copper town – each house standing amid a generous allowance of cultivated green lawn, whose rich colour and texture are a tribute to the all-year-round watering which the dull, dust-coated bush grass does not receive.

Dominating the town is the headgear of one of the great mines, etched sharply against the intense blue sky. Drive on through the town and within minutes it has vanished completely, swallowed up in Africa. The first encounter with a copper town has a dream-like quality, as though you had seen a mirage of Hampstead or Cheam transposed to the heart of Africa – a shimmering fantasy induced by the oppressive heat and rarefied air. The highway thrusts on, usually as straight as a die, to the next town and the next, until it peters out into a dirt track which ends at a customs post, with its inevitable general store and police post. Beyond is the vast, empty, mysterious hinterland of the Congo.

A bare half-century ago the tiny slice of Northern

Rhodesia which is now this El Dorado slept. A few Africans wandered through the bush, but not many, since the main locations of the great tribes of the country were hundreds of miles distant. Only the Lala and the Lamba, two minor tribes, claimed this area as their home. Elephant and buffalo abounded, the one attracted by the bamboo shoots which sprang up around the thin trees, and the other by the matete bushes.

The discovery of the area that was to become known as the Copperbelt, the Commonwealth's second largest producer of the metal, is one of the most romantic stories to emerge from Africa. One day in 1902 a prospector named William Collier shot a roan antelope feeding by a river bank. As he strolled up to prepare it for his supper he noticed that its head lay against a rock stained green with copper. A quarter of a century later the Roan Antelope Copper Mine was built on that spot, a mighty monument to a providential shot. The peace of Lambaland was at an end.

The *abasungu*[1] came, first with prospector's picks, then with bulldozers and locomotives. Soon the Copperbelt was a magnet for the adventurous and the unemployed from South Africa, Canada, and Britain. It became cosmopolitan, unique – and engendered within itself totally artificial social standards. The pioneers could not be blamed. With sweat, blood, often their lives, they created a miracle of which they were justifiably proud, and which they jealously determined to preserve. Isolated as they were, it is small wonder that their awareness of what was happening on the other side of the oceans of bush became distorted. They set a pattern that became a heritage for following generations of immigrant miners – the belief that the Copperbelt was for the White man, because White brains and investment and technical know-how had created it (which, in purely material terms, was true). That Black brawn had also contributed was never given a second thought; indeed, it hardly mattered, for at that time the African was not imbued with the tiniest flicker of political consciousness. The

[1]White man.

15

militant march of African nationalism was in the folded future.

Northern Rhodesia was – and, as Zambia, is – abjectly dependent on copper. To exploit the metal, the mining companies had to provide social facilities superior to those offered anywhere else – a tall order considering the Copperbelt's remoteness. They created towns, built highways, eradicated malaria and other sub-tropical scourges, raised magnificently-equipped hospitals, and offered within the restricted boundaries of communities little larger than an English village everything necessary for a good life.

The picture of the White settler spending his unoccupied hours in a rocking chair on the *stoep* of his house, a glass of whisky in his hand, listening to the night sounds of Africa and dreaming nostalgically of home, belongs to the works of Somerset Maugham. The Nchanga miner, like his counterparts at other mines, could take his choice between first-class sports fields and swimming pools, a magnificent golf course claimed by Bobby Locke to be the finest in Africa, an air-conditioned cinema and an opulent club which had everything from a full-sized ballroom to well-stocked bars. The lavishness of the social services provided by the mining companies was also symbolized by the Nchanga Mine Hospital – seventy beds and staffed by a specialist surgeon, radiologist, six medical officers, and thirty fully-qualified nursing sisters – this for a town of four thousand European inhabitants, three quarters of whom were wives and families of the miners.

Nor had African workers been overlooked. As individual mines expanded and the Copperbelt took shape, so also grew African townships built by the companies. Thousands of Africans flocked in to claim their share of the untold wealth beneath the earth. There sprang up endless rows of small houses, lighted streets, welfare centres, beer gardens and football stadia, together with a comprehensive health service providing everything that European employees could boast.

Those who have seen something of the squalor and

poverty of the rural African would not be inclined to judge this all-embracing welfare policy as the epitome of Victorian paternalism, though the charge has often been levelled at the mining companies. African miners were decently housed, ate well, were taken care of in sickness, and earned wages which enabled at least the wise among them to live well-founded lives and give their children a fighting chance of a good education.

Yet for all their spaciousness, the copper towns were under stress. Because of their artificial origins and physical remoteness, they abounded in personal and social problems which made total demands upon the clergy, doctors and welfare workers. Paradoxically, the very effortlessness of life was a major cause of personal maladjustment.

Morris summed it up in *The Hour After Midnight*[1].

'If, as the psychologist claims, human character matures through the challenge of hardship, then there is little doubt that the solicitous attention, bottomless purse and perpetually smoothed path which represents the influence of the copper companies upon the communities they dominate weakens moral backbone and saps the will of people to cope with those ethical and psychological problems which are beyond the range of the companies' benevolence.'

Simply, the communities were rootless. In them, men and women were pitilessly exposed to all the pressures of life without the protection of long-standing traditions, established ways of doing things, and the nurture of the wider family circle. Many Copperbelt Europeans lived like residents of a fabulous Land of Begin Again. Battered by experiences in other places, and attracted by the promise of quick wealth and physical remoteness, they had made their pilgrimage into the wilderness, leaving all behind them except their major handicap – themselves.

The Copperbelt had the indefinable aura of the boarding house about it. Few of its people were permanent residents, content to end their days in the territory. Most White

[1] Longmans Green, London, 1961.

17

copper miners lived and worked for the day when they would leave Northern Rhodesia for ever, substantial gratuities in their pockets, and retire to a farm in South Africa, a little business in Aberdeen or a house by the sea at Bognor Regis.

There was another undercurrent of tension about which Morris then, for all practical purposes, knew nothing – Race. Black Africa was on the march. In the African townships at Chingola and other towns there were the first faint stirrings of discontent as the men of Northern Rhodesia's seventy or so tribes discovered a hitherto unknown unity of purpose which far and wide smashed down inter-tribal barriers. It was discontentment soon to be sharpened by news of tremendous political happenings in other colonial territories.

Long subdued, pliant, and unquestioning of their inferior status, Africans – suddenly, it seemed – began to see Race in the same sharp terms as Europeans: Blacks and Whites with ne'er a tinge of grey. Their mutterings grew louder, their tempers warmer, and their frustrations more keenly felt. A parallel might be found in Bulwer Lytton's graphic description, in his *Last Days of Pompeii*, of a cultured, gay community pursuing the even tenor of its privileged way, sublimely unaware that the sleeping volcano in whose lee it nestled was about to erupt into destructive life.

That was the Copperbelt in 1956.

A man and a time coalesced. Ten years earlier, Colin Morris's thunderous utterances would have echoed hollowly in a political vacuum. Ten years later the struggle was over – Zambians ruled their own land and had no need of a White champion. But Central Africa in 1956 was when and where the action was. And one of the focal points became the pulpit of Chingola Free Church.

2

COLIN MORRIS settled into his tin-roofed manse, somewhat intimidated by its spaciousness, having graduated from a Lancashire two-up and two-down via a Marine barracks to an Oxford bed-sitter. He hired, and fired, his first servants, going through the process common to most newcomers to Africa of treating them initially with fond indulgence until the quantities of disappearing sugar, teaspoons, and handkerchiefs threatened to paralyse his life and called for stern action. Eventually, after a succession of adventures with the more plausible rogues of the servant fraternity, he placed himself in the hands of an old cook called George who knew every trick in the book but at least, when sober, was reasonably reliable. He also invested in an Alsatian pup called Liz, for the company. He chose Liz as a pet; later she was to become his fierce defender. But in those sunny early days he could not have foreseen the need for any protection more lethal than a fly spray.

Chingola Free Church was only a name on a notice board. The congregation, all twenty of them, met in the local community hall and sang hymns to a tinny piano played by the local dance band pianist. They were a motley crew of Methodists, Congregationalists, and Presbyterians. One mistake the early missionaries to the Copperbelt did not make was to establish Churches that reflected the denominational divisions back home.

Grave doubts had been expressed in the Chingola Free Church Council about the comparative youth of the new minister. Traditionally, new missionaries were stationed in remote bush locations and only graduated to the towns along the line of rail as a reward for long service. Morris's predecessor, the Rev. Douglas Gray, was a pioneer missionary who had arrived in Northern Rhodesia before the first World War, established a number of mission stations including the famous Chipembi Girls' School – for a long time the only secondary school for African girls in the country – and spent the final years of a distinguished career graciously ministering to the Chingola congregation, who adored him. In 1962, Colin Morris dedicated one of his most provocative books *The End of the Missionary?* to Douglas Gray as from 'One who stands aghast at his achievements'.

Morris's first sermons convinced the congregation that neither his youth nor his Oxford background were likely to be much of a handicap in getting on to the wavelength of a tough mining community. After all, he had grown up in a working class community, made up largely of Lancashire coal miners who could teach even Copperbelters a thing or two when it came to rumbustuous living. 'At least he can preach!' conceded Arthur Short, the Church Secretary, a somewhat dour Congregationalist with an inbred suspicion of Methodists, as he left the community hall after Morris's first service.

Expending fantastic energy in building up his congregation and making an impact upon the little town, Morris soon had his Church Council planning a permanent home for the congregation. A site was purchased, a £20,000 church designed, and the foundations dug. Thus far, Morris conformed exactly to the standard image of the go-ahead young parson, dashing around, busily roping in newcomers to swell his growing congregation.

It might all have been happening in Manchester or the southern suburbs of London. The forty thousand Africans who lived in compounds on the outskirts of Chingola went about their predestined courses hardly ever impinging on the lives of the White settlers, except when they cycled whistling out of their townships every morning to put in a day's work for their White masters, and then retreated at

20

sundown to their infinitely remote and self-contained world on the wrong side of the colour line.

It was in 1956 that African Christians became for the first time bitterly articulate about the colour bar in the European Churches of Northern Rhodesia. Shortly after Morris's arrival in Chingola a crisis developed on his doorstep. Two prominent members of his church stalked out of his Induction Service in a fury because half a dozen Elders of an African sister-church had been invited to attend. And a handful of European members, catching sight of this row of rather self-conscious and poorly-dressed African Christians turned away without entering the church. This distressing happening signalled a warning to Morris about the strength of his congregation's feelings on racial mixing. Old-timers, concerned to educate him about the facts of life in Africa, also subjected him to a mélange of tales, compounded of myth, half-truth and contemptuous recital, about the backwardness, perfidy and insanitariness of the African in his natural habitat.

He listened in amazement as his well-meaning people told him of the time that an African policeman attending Holy Communion in the local Anglican Church had been taken ill with a disease subsequently diagnosed as leprosy. 'There you are!' exclaimed European opinion triumphantly 'That is the risk you run when Africans sit next to you in Church.' The fact that leprosy, contrary to popular belief, is not a contagious disease, and that Europeans go down every day with nasty infections caught by contact with other Europeans, was neither here nor there. European fears had been vindicated. Close proximity between the races must have the most horrid consequences.

Those Africans Morris did meet showed little evidence of writhing under the hardships of the colour bar. At Oxford he had met only the intense, bitter, articulate African political leaders, imported by courtesy of the Africa Bureau to address the various undergraduate societies and seminars whose special interest was the Federation of Rhodesia and

Nyasaland. One of the first contradictions that struck Morris in Chingola was the stark contrast between the obvious misery of these visitors to Britain and the irrepressible gaiety of their brothers 'at home'. Their electric smiles, alternating indolence and vibrant energy, their songs and dances, zest for living, all combined to make apparent mockery of the heated concern of their political champions abroad. Oppression? Exploitation? Morris studied the sunny smiles and found no clues. Only in time would he learn that there was nothing incongruous between the leisurely lives and the driving political ambition of Northern Rhodesia Africans, for it was only time – combined with the trust afforded him by African friends – that allowed him a glimpse of the heartache and despair that lay beneath their gay exteriors.

But, at the outset, he did not know any Africans; he noticed only their public front. What he saw filled him with roseate reassurance rather than dark foreboding. Unwittingly, he allowed himself to be drawn into the trap of thinking *White*. It was all part of his apprenticeship. One of the burdens on his conscience today is that for almost a year he found himself, though not without reserve, in common accord with colonial thought processes.

Why, asked Morris, should Africans aspire to enter White bars, restaurants, clubs and cinemas, and to desert the sunny conviviality of their own communities? The segregation of White and Black in the Federation seemed a fact of life easily justifiable on the grounds of convenience and culture.

Any unease about the failings and mistakes of colonials in Africa was quieted by the eminent reasonableness of his new friends. Those who, overseas, represented them as devils incarnate were not only doing them an injustice but were missing completely the true essence of the situation being played out in the Federation as a whole. These Europeans were neither better nor worse than their counterparts in any other society. And when, stung by the criticisms of the British and American newspapers, they flung back

Notting Hill and Little Rock in the faces of overseas opinion, there was much point to their rejoinder.

Of this period, the twilight of the Federation's brief era, Morris wrote:

'Were the inhabitants of any British or American town to be transplanted in Central Africa there are no grounds for assuming that they would make a better job of the racial situation here. White Rhodesians are ordinary folk who have appeared on the stage of history in time to grapple with a problem which would daunt the wisdom of Plato's Philosopher-Kings. And one of the reasons why it is easy to misjudge them is that whereas their mistakes are painfully obvious to the outside world, their sincerity can only be appreciated by those on the spot.'

He had been prepared to dislike White settlers intensely, for propaganda had assured him that they were the Bad Side in the melodrama of Central Africa. He had been totally disarmed. They did not stalk about the place arrogantly, tapping rhino whips against their boots. They did not kick Africans off the pavements nor beat up their house servants. On the contrary, with the inevitable exceptions, they treated the Africans who worked for them with a paternal concern which Morris found touching.

He did not then see the situation for what it really was, feudalism all over again – the lord of the manor and his peasants establishing an easy, informal relationship within the framework of a static social order, each one instinctively knowing his place. These pleasant relationships were to dissolve as the Race tempo quickened, being replaced by sullenness on the one side and suspicion on the other. The peasant was becoming a threat to the manorial lord.

On a personal plane Morris was unhappy to find that he had not the knack of some other missionaries of establishing easy, informal relationships with Africans. He felt acutely uncomfortable in their presence. His own conclusion was that he lacked both the social grace to assume a cordiality towards them he did not feel, and the humility to see that there was something to be gained in a closer relationship.

The few educated Africans he did meet were without the poise and maturity of West African intellectuals he had known at Oxford, who, with their pedantic English, charcoal-grey suits, and the inevitable brief case (or alternatively walking stick) seemed caricatures of the suburbanites who packed the morning train to Paddington.

Nor did he like the arrogance and contempt some of them showed to their less advanced brothers. Two who visited him at the manse ordered his servants around in strident tones which Morris had never heard the most reactionary European use to address an African.

Yet he was bound to admit to himself that his own racial arrogance, try as he might to curb it, was causing him to demand the impossible of the African people. Product of an aggressive civilization which since the Industrial Revolution has based its standards upon success, efficiency, and superficial refinement, he weighed his early African acquaintances in the scales against these standards and found them wanting.

Still, as a duty, he went along to the handful of multi-racial clubs and activities which enjoyed a lukewarm vogue on the Copperbelt. He found these first tentative experiments in partnership disillusioning and, to his mind, a complete waste of time. Those in attendance draped themselves around a room, cups of tea perched on their knees, and laughed over-heartily at each other's weak jokes, grimly determined to be all pals together.

Morris recalls:

'We trod delicately around any of the issues which were a real cause of difference and went home exhausted from the effort of trying to pretend that there was the slightest common ground between us. We listened to talks which ranged from African Tribal Customs to My Visit to England; whilst the European members expounded on Jam Making, the Cultivation of Cacti and Missionary Work in China. It was all terribly nice and

24

utterly futile, as we discovered when the membership dwindled to nothing. All that remained was a couple of pounds in the bank and a glaring moral – that mere physical contact between the races proves nothing and solves nothing in itself.'

One reason for the failure of such 'cultural' clubs was that they were launched by those agencies – the Churches, the municipal councils and the Big Brother copper mines – so generally terrified of controversy that they banned all the subjects which were likely to lead to that cut and thrust of conflicting opinion which is a genuine form of contact. Equally important, Africans and Europeans were just not prepared to be absolutely honest with each other for the sake of truth. Their self-conscious politeness was a subtle form of racial discrimination; there was not between them that brutal frankness which is one of the characteristics of true friendship.

Morris went about his business as the fairly popular and successful minister of a growing church. He rejoiced particularly in his congregation's opinion of him as a hard-headed realist where racial matters were concerned. They compared him, to his credit, with 'dangerous' men like Canon John Collins, who, they claimed, was unable to open his mouth in the pulpit without thundering doom on the White settlers of southern Africa from a position of comfortable remoteness. There is ironic humour in the fact that four years later he was being compared with Canon Collins to the worthy Canon's credit. Wrote one correspondent to the *Northern News*, the country's leading daily:

'I note that Canon Collins has had the good sense to stop trying to solve the problems of Central Africa from the centre of London, and is now concerning himself with the H-Bomb – a real problem about which the Church should be much more outspoken. I do not recall having read that Chingola's 'Turbulent Priest' has publicly condemned nuclear weapons. He should follow

25

the Rev. Collins' example and stop making the African people discontented with their lot through his fiery sermons. . . . .'

His church was filling nicely. He liked his White Rhodesian congregation and did not want to lose any of them, so six months after his arrival in Africa he rose to his feet in the Northern Rhodesia Methodist Synod to oppose a motion calling for racial integration in Church services and throughout the community generally. The conditioning process was complete. In a long and angry speech he put forward arguments which many clergy and ministers in areas of racial tension find convincing today and which determine their racial policies. For this reason they are worth recording.

In the first place, it seemed foolhardy for the minister of a European church to thunder doom upon his congregation for their unwillingness to fraternize with Africans. Surely there was only one way to get people to change their views on an issue as fundamental as this, and that was to win them to a greater love and understanding for the members of other races by slow and painstaking persuasion. But to do this one would have to make common ground with them and get their confidence and trust. A rigorous and unyielding stand on the Race issue would undoubtedly drive them out of the Church, and once this happened they would be completely beyond the sphere of one's influence. They could be reached neither by preaching nor by persuasion. And what seemed to him worse, in their bitterness at having been, as they thought, excluded from the Fellowship, they would hate Africans all the more. The net result would be the loss of a fair slice of the congregation and an increase in racial tension.

Was the right attitude to Race a necessary condition of salvation? Was liberalism part of the essence of the Gospel, or was it not one of those ethical outworkings about which there could be legitimately conflicting views, as in the case of drink, gambling, and divorce? If a parson continually forced pacifism down the throats of his congregation until those who were unable to accept that position left the

Church, the condemnation he would bring upon himself would be universal and deserved. Where did the issue of Race differ?

The preacher's primary task, surely, was to offer his congregation the Gospel, not to foist upon them what amounted to a semi-political programme for Central Africa, or to make his personal view of a controversial issue mandatory for membership of his Church. Anyway, who dared say that integration was necessarily and always the right attitude to Race?

He concluded with a ringing call for patience and forbearance. Wisdom decreed that they should wait until the gap between the races had narrowed through an increase in African education and a decrease in European prejudice before trying to throw a bridge across the racial chasm. There was a natural time for coming together, and that time would be determined by history.

Morris's powerful advocacy carried the day and a suitably non-committal compromise resolution was passed, calculated to upset no one – no one, that is, except the rows of weary African ministers who had heard it all before and despaired of the Church ever putting its house in order. Few, if any, of those Black saints present that day would have predicted that within six months the fiery oratory of this same missionary would be deployed in smashing down the Church's colour bar once and for all.

3

IN the meantime Colin Morris was fast gaining a reputation as a controversialist by his pragmatic treatment from the pulpit of such stock-in-trade subjects as sex, drink, hire-purchase habits and the like. They were not so much outrageous in content as provocative in their hard realism. And they made all the more impact because of Morris's gift for presenting them in technicolour language. His approach was deliberately *Daily Mirror* rather than *Telegraph* – and his utterings were eagerly recorded by Central African newspapers: 'We all have a bit of the Old Nick in us. That's what makes us assume the police are our dearest enemies and not our closest friends' . . . 'If people make the golf club or the pub their church, then they should get the professional to marry them or the barman to baptise them.'

Nor did he scruple to attack powerful targets. Thus, Mayoral Sunday. Present were His Worship the Mayor, resplendent in ermine; Mr Town Clerk, bewigged and begowned; Councillors, almost penguin-like in their best blacks and greys; the First Lady and other wives, as pretty-hatted as possible from the limited range offered by the mining town's only departmental store.

It was gloriously bright weather, typical of Northern Rhodesia and the perfect backdrop to the pomp of an important day. Chingola Free Church, recently dedicated and still clinical in its whitewash and pastels, was being honoured for the first time as the religious stage for this annual civic service. The anonymous ladies who create much of the atmosphere of any church with their flower arrangements had surpassed themselves, and the church plate, burnished copper, positively gleamed. Likely enough it had, in its raw state, enriched the very earth on which the new building stood.

The Town Clerk led their Worships and the procession to the front pews. Relatives and friends took their places alongside regular members of the congregation. The organist played a few discreet chords to set the mood and to remind Morris, robing in his vestry, that he was awaited.

Probably every city and town in the English-speaking world upholds this traditional confrontation between local council and God through the medium of the local church. Invariably it is the church of whoever happens to be Mayor's Chaplain for that year, and so it was on this occasion – Mayor James Fleming being a Free Church worshipper.

Yet, truth be known, Mr Fleming had shown some courage in choosing Morris's church for this particular service. Some of his predecessors, although non-conformist, and therefore nominally in Morris's parish, had 'gone' Anglican or Catholic (in the loosest sense) for their terms of office rather than associate with this young minister, a few years out from England, whose sermons and activities were somewhat loud-check for their small-town mentalities.

Mayor Fleming had no such inhibitions, though it can be assumed that he had to resist certain anti-Morris pressures when deciding on the venue. To his credit, he placed valour before discretion. If his Council was to receive God's blessing for its Christian endeavours on behalf of local citizens, then there was no question of it being conferred anywhere else than at the Chingola Free Church.

Morris rewarded his show of integrity with a verbal kick in the teeth – a public tongue-lashing that had the Mayor and his council squirming with embarrassment on pews that had never felt so hard.

From the pulpit he thundered: 'I hope you have not come here expecting a pat on the back for the public spirited work you are doing. Take a look at our town. Not the spacious, tree-lined avenues where we and our kind luxuriate but the crowded, insanitary hovels where the Black citizens of this town eke out a miserable existence. They are your care, too, and a fat lot you've done for them. I was tempted to read my lesson not from the Bible but from the Municipal Treasurer's Annual Report so that we could boast before God about the way we have stewarded our town's wealth. Let's sing praises unto the Lord about the fact that we have spent eight times more money on amenities for 1,000 Whites than for 30,000 Africans. If we have no intention of taking the faith of Jesus seriously then let's not troop into God's House on ceremonial occasions but rather declare ourselves honest pagans.'

Morris was not attacking Mayor Fleming personally or, necessarily, any other individual serving on the Council. He was pounding, with an aggressiveness that was to become accepted as commonplace, the belief of nearly all White settlers in Northern Rhodesia that it was *their* country by virtue of the White pioneering that had dragged it and its peoples into the twentieth century.

This one-sided, totally invalid argument was based upon the premise that the African, deemed to be at least two hundred years behind any European standard, could 'never catch up'; hence he was a second-class citizen whose rôle could only be servitude. The die had been cast at first meeting between pith helmet and loin cloth at the end of the nineteenth century.

Morris saw a glaring reflection of this attitude in the condition of Chingola's municipal African township, or, grotesque misnomer, compound, at Kasompe. Subjected to near-total neglect because of the official blind eye, it had degenerated into what he termed 'original Hell'. He was horrified at the sight of dozens of families sharing one communal tap, of blocked latrines and overflowing sewers, of the flies and mosquitoes that inevitably thrived in the absence of regular visits by disinfectant-spray teams. Running repairs to the decrepit dwellings were carried out by residents with patchwork quilts of old linoleum and corrugated iron sheeting, the only weather-proofing they could afford on wages that averaged eight pounds a month – this in a country which, because of its landlocked position in southern Africa, has a very high cost of living. Chingola Council's township maintenance programme, seemingly generous when viewed in the Town Treasurer's expenditure reports, was considerably behind schedule. And no one was hurrying. There were more urgent things to attend to on the European side of town.

The general White outlook was that Africans themselves were totally responsible for the hygiene and tidiness of their townships, in any normal situation a valid argument. Overlooked in this case was that, just as with Glasgow's Gorbals district of yesteryear, the means for attainment of reasonable standards had first to be supplied by the authorities. Even today, many Europeans in the country sneer at African standards of living despite available proof that, given the incentive, residents of an African township can emulate anything European. Of course there are many who don't even try – just as there are many Europeans whose standards are considerably lower than those of Africans about whom they complain.

A good example of African response to provision of 'European-type' homes in which to live is at the Orchard township in Mufulira, one of Chingola's neighbouring towns on the ninety-mile-long banana-shaped Copperbelt. It bears any scrutiny, and the reason is not hard to find. Its residents were given conditions worth cherishing and preserving: decent houses on good sized plots of land, tarred roads instead of rutted tracks outside their front fences, adequate plumbing, electric lighting, and dustbins, and a regular maintenance programme. The pride of tenancy among residents is as marked as in any of Britain's stockbroker belts, even if some of the ex-villager housewives who took occupancy of these modern homes had to be taught simple things like the correct use of a broom. But patience and genuine concern in helping such people step from yesterday into today won through, just as Morris

31

knew it could. The difference was that he was voicing the claim more than a decade before most other Europeans. In emergent Africa, ten years seems a lifetime.

Naturally Morris hit the headlines over the civic service. Such a crossing of swords with a public body and the manner in which it was done made it inevitable. And in subsequent months he lashed out on any social matter which grated upon his strong socialistic conscience. His name and headlines became synonymous, as they still are. Reports of his utterances were not confined to Northern Rhodesia. Newspapers, as well as governmental departments, were closely linked in the three territories of the Federation, and accounts of his sermons were also read in the neighbouring capitals of Salisbury, Southern Rhodesia, and Blantyre, Nyasaland. Eyebrows in high places were raised, and mental notes made that tabs would need to be kept on this newcomer if he continued in present vein. The Federal Government, led by Sir Roy Welensky, had from its Salisbury base ultimate control over the three territories, and had enough problems selling its 'partnership' policy to Africans without eloquent denunciators of their own colour selling the pass.

Morris remained resolute. He was at first quite unable to identify himself with the common feeling of abhorrence to everything Black, though he was fully aware that it was expected of him. The only concession, if such it was, he would make was to exercise a certain discretion on the central issue of Race and thus save the feelings of his congregation.

White settlers were determined to re-make the country in their own image and were so cocksure of their racial superiority that they would call an African civilized only if his behaviour and speech were faithful imitations of their own. Not that Europeans treated Africans as beasts of burden or with studied brutality. The assaults were of a more insidious nature – arrogant monopoly of the right to judge, by standards of their own choosing, the humanity and

32

civilized worth of those whose skin pigmentation was different from their own.

Morris did not deliberately set out to gain reportage, and the fact that he was subjected to it embarrassed him initially. Later, however, he was to become an adept at 'using' the press by commanding its attention whenever it suited his propaganda purposes. Like so many other public figures, he learned of the enormous power of newspapers in swaying or dictating public opinion. Without qualms, and not worrying about his clerical dignity, he took full advantage of the medium with a strategy that would have done credit to any highly trained press officer.

Years later Morris told his interviewer in a televised Face-to-Face programme:

'It is probably true that I am a publicity seeker and I make no apology for the fact. Why should I preach to a hundred or a couple of hundred when, through press and radio, I can get my views across to thousands of people who will never come within range of my unaided voice? I am, as a preacher, a publicist, a purveyor of ideas – the saving truths of the Gospel. And, frankly, I could not worry less why people come to Church, whether through vulgar curiosity or for any other reason. As long as the message I preach is not merely stuntery but the truth, then I am not disposed to worry about being labelled a publicity seeker or pulpit stunt merchant. Any number of people have come to Church for the wrong reason and gone away with the right message. That is the important thing.'

There is a clue to the Morris make-up in the phrase '. . . get *my* views across . . .', and he would be the last to deny that he has always felt a driving need to broadcast himself as widely as possible on pertinent matters. Here the egoist is suspected; but Morris is adamant that he has never sought publicity for its own sake, or to gain any personal stimulation. 'In all humility, I have always honestly felt that I had something useful to contribute by way of ideas. Mind you, I have also committed my fair share of blunders. Per-

33

haps the worst was that, early on, I tended to rush into print too often.'

No doubt part of his instinctive desire to speak out is the result of boyhood conditioning when, as the 'baby' of a family of much older sisters, he was virtually weaned on adult conversation and thinking, and encouraged to say his piece. Certainly there was little irrelevant activity in the Morris household in Bolton, Lancashire, for it was a regular meeting place for overalled intellectuals from the mining world in which his father was a trade union official. It is also worth noting that Morris's grandfather was a firebrand member of the soapbox brigade, orating every Sunday afternoon on Bolton's Town Hall steps, and that Morris himself cut his oratorical teeth in soapbox parliaments. Words have always been one of the dominant factors of his life. As a boy, they were his playthings; as an adult, his passion.

He evoked laughter, clicking tongues, the suspicion of religious traditionalists, and a measure of enmity from some fellow churchmen. Criticism did not upset him. If some people were aggravated by his 'playing to the gallery', Morris at least had the satisfaction of a full church – a rarity on the Copperbelt of those days. Though he got a kick from the whole business, his basic motivation was concern for attracting people to church. Having done so, he could do no more than hope they would become regular worshippers.

Morris was undismayed at charges from some quarters that he was acting like a Barnum and turning his church into a kind of circus. He was convinced that if he was to perform his ministry effectively he had to adopt methods suitable to the situation and the mentality of the public at large. And it *was* an unusual mentality with which to deal. Pulpit 'performers' might be ten a penny in Britain, but colonials, hell-raisers in most other things, expected in their parsons a formality which reminded them of their younger days in the Old Country.

He also caught the attention of the newspapers over the

case of a man suffering cancer, who was given a 'death sentence' by his doctor. Morris's first association with the tragedy was when the man's wife banged at his door and, distraught, gabbled that her husband had put a hosepipe in his car and driven off into the dense bush that surrounds Chingola.

The frantic wife had first rushed to the police station, but colonial officers there did not seem interested in the fact that a man was bent on suicide in preference to a lingering death.

Morris immediately commandeered an aircraft from the local flying club and began to comb the area from the air. He searched for days without success; it was like looking for the proverbial needle. Forced to give up the air search, he then organized a flying squad of cars driven by Church members and, days later, the man's car was found. Its blackened interior told only too clearly his fate.

The following Sunday Morris had some uncomplimentary remarks to make about the casual attitude of the local police. He made them loudly and clearly from the pulpit. Needless to say, the police were not amused.

A Sunday newspaperman coined the nickname 'the Flying Parson' in reporting the incident, and the name stuck until he became politically active in 1960. Then, following the publication of a cartoon in the *African Times* depicting Morris in the ring delivering a straight left to the ex-pugilist Sir Roy Welensky, it was adulterated to the Fighting Parson. And Fighting Parson, a title which has never ceased to embarrass him with its mock heroic overtones, he has been dubbed ever since. All Morris's pleas to his press friends to drop this sobriquet which he detested fell on deaf ears. To them he represented the ministry at its most untypical and militant – and anyway, 'Fighting Parson' made for snappy headlines:

'The Fighting Parson Strikes Again.'
'The Fighting Parson K.O.s Welensky In
Synod Federation Resolution . . .'
and 'Fighting Parson Counted Out!' when
he fell ill.

People came to expect every one of his sermons to offer 'entertainment' as opposed to uplift. Morris was deeply upset that some people tended to overlook his basic seriousness of purpose merely because he happened to have acquired a catchy nickname. He resolved to be more discreet in ensuing months when dealing with topical social subjects.

'I went by the textbook!' he recalls – though newspaper cuttings of the time show this recollection to be not entirely correct. In fact, some little time after this, an editorial in the *Northern News* observed:

> 'The church militant is something we seldom see or hear of, and yet opportunities for leadership of this kind are certainly not lacking. It seems to us that in this way it would best attract and retain the fealty of men of goodwill, ability and character. We are, of course, generalizing. We need go no further than Chingola to find the Reverend Colin Morris, a minister who goes well beyond the usual field of church subjects. We believe the voice of religion should be clearer and louder in the councils of the land.'

4

THE *Northern News* was pleading for 'the voice of religion
to be heard clearer and louder'. It got its wish when Morris,
in an early burst of confidence, took on a giant adversary –
the Anglo American Corporation – and involved himself in
its decision to close the Bancroft Mine.

Bancroft, sixteen miles from Chingola and not a large
mine by Copperbelt standards, was opened in 1956 shortly
after Morris's arrival in the country. Two years later, the
A.A.C., which controlled two huge Copperbelt mines as
well as having enormous investments in many other parts of
Africa and beyond, decided to close Bancroft because of a
drop in the demand for copper.

The mine employed comparatively few Europeans,
easily absorbed by other mines. But for thousands of African
workers, mostly labourers, it was a different story. They had
arrived from the rural areas for their first contact with an
industrial environment and its attendant material luxuries,
and they naturally wanted to stay. For the first time in their
lives they had the chance of living in the twentieth century
– a chance suddenly snatched away.

The Anglo American Corporation felt itself unable or
under no obligation to resettle the Africans on other mines,
while the Northern Rhodesia Legislative Council demurred
at suggestions that it should find alternative, non-mining
work for them. Other large industrial groups, aware of a
growing Copperbelt unemployment problem, maintained a
tactful silence. It looked as though the Africans at Bancroft
were no one's problem.

Morris made them his. Speaking angrily from his pulpit he
said:

'The Bancroft closure means a return to the Dark Ages for all these men. It is the end of their hopes of educating their children and sharing in the exciting new life of the towns. It is pointless to deny that the African population has derived considerable benefits from the enterprise of the copper companies, but, however sound the economics of the closure, it has first to be judged by the Christian in terms of its effect on human beings.'

One effect was, of course, to fan the flames of bitterness more and more Africans were feeling towards White Settlers. Morris asked:

'Having for a rich profit introduced these Africans into a new life with exciting possibilities, is the industry's responsibility towards them discharged by providing them with a good breakfast and a one-way ticket back to the bush? If it is, then the sooner the system is changed, and its place taken by one where human destiny is no longer at the mercy of the market, the better.'

A few liberally-minded applauded his argument. But the majority of Whites claimed he was throwing religion out of the window and giving vent to his deep-rooted socialism. Public opinion did not bother him overmuch. He may have sensed that the basis of their criticism was the simple fact that he had dared to speak out on behalf of the *kaffirs*, or *munts* as local parlance had it, but it is clear that he had no idea at this time of getting involved in the racial struggle. He defended them because they were workers victimized by Big Business, not because they were Blacks suffering at the hands of Whites.

Wrote Mr Eric Clayton, Chairman of the Bancroft Branch of the European Mine Workers' Union, in the *Northern News*: 'Mr Morris is bringing further disrepute on a pulpit already burdened by his peculiar views. Obviously he intends to forsake his mission in the cause of Christianity and further his own interests in a political or trade union field.'

If the charge that he would be prepared to forsake his mission was an unkind cut, the rest of the letter was an uncannily correct forecast, all the more so as Morris is adamant that at the time nothing was further from his mind than entry into politics.

In attacking the mining companies Morris was truly playing David confronting Goliath. One of the first things he had heard on arriving in Chingola was the statement 'the Companies won't like it', the implication being that they were some kind of irresistible power. It did not pay to get across them.

Though not above the law in its strictest sense, the companies wielded enormous influence in many fields, not least governmental. Indeed, a number of their employees were members of the Legislature as well as of local councils, the latter on a nominee basis. Appreciating that copper was the backbone of the country and that almost every aspect of the economy was affected by either the ebb or flow of its fortunes on world markets, it is not hard to see the scope of their influence. They held the purse strings, and it was true that they took care of employees from birth to death. Should his life span be short enough, it was possible for a child first to see the light of the world in the maternity wing of a Mine Hospital and, as an adult, make his last journey in a coffin provided by the Company.

It was inevitable that the companies emerged as, collectively, a Golden Cow whose benign approval and financial help everyone sought. Not that they ever proved ungenerous – over the years they poured millions of pounds into the Territory.

But if the companies never openly applied pressure to a group or individual, they were quite capable of making life uncomfortable for anyone who gained their disapproval. Morris was often to have a taste of this treatment, usually in the form of being snubbed or, for varying periods, 'sent to Coventry' by individual managements. He was more exhilarated than upset by the disapproval of the industrial Powers-that-Be; this was the old class war bred into his bones and absorbed with his mother's milk in depression-hit Lancashire. This was one war he did understand, even if

39

the ramifications of the racial issue puzzled him.

Fast in the wake of the Bancroft episode was a strike by European miners which paralysed the Copperbelt for two months. Morris, having gained powerful enemies on the employer side of the industry through the Bancroft issue, now presented his other cheek by lambasting the Whites' union and, for the second time in weeks, the mining companies.

The European union enjoyed a power which belied its membership of a mere 5,000. It had been formed in 1938 and at the time of the 1958 crisis was at the zenith of a power vested in the fact that its members were the technicians of the mines. They jealously guarded a closed-shop agreement with the companies which had been obtained during the Second World War when copper was a vital asset to the Allied effort. The union made its demand for a closed-shop privilege at a time when the companies were in no position to bargain; production *had* to be maintained, whatever the arguments between employers and workers. In fact, the companies were so preoccupied with maintaining copper output that they raised hardly a bleat. Future years gave them great cause for regret at their compliance.

The 1958 strike followed a healthy period when the miners' annual copper bonus, based on the state of the market and other considerations, reached an all-time peak of one hundred and eight per cent. This meant that a man earning, say, a basic £100 a month also received £108 bonus for that month. Fantastic sums were picked up by some of the White miners. One rockbreaker in one month earned £800 through the footage he achieved, a figure doubled by the high bonus. In subsequent years the bonus dropped to the forty to sixty per cent region before being discontinued altogether. After this particularly prosperous year the companies decided to transfer a number of jobs to African workers which, claimed the Europeans, were reserved to them through the closed-shop agreement. None of these jobs required much skill and the White union was also upset because the companies intended paying the Africans

40

much less than their own members had been paid. This they claimed, was adding insult to injury, and a strike ensued.

The shutdown dragged into its seventh week, putting the whole Copperbelt under considerable strain. Commerce, reliant on miners' money, also faced great problems. Tempers were short, and many wild statements and threats were bandied about – not least one from an anonymous group who threatened to drop bombs down the mine shafts and 'teach the companies a lesson'.

Morris, having closely studied the situation and kept silence as long as his impetuous nature would allow, finally gave vent in a packed church. His sermon gained the main headline in every one of the Federation's newspapers next morning. He became the whipping boy everyone was looking for, someone on whom all and sundry could, under the guise of 'fair game', turn and pour out their spite and frustration. His sermon, presented in his usual uncompromising manner, caused a furore which almost resulted in his being blown right out of Northern Rhodesia.

From the pulpit he claimed that, stripped of its technicalities, the dispute resolved itself into a conflict of interests between the companies and the union which could never be reconciled. He saw the companies' move as part of a plan of revenge in the light of the now regretted closed-shop concession, and the union's attitude as one of deep-seated fear that loss of control over jobs would sooner or later lead to the displacement of their members in favour of Africans.

The unbiased, what few there were, agreed that Morris had accurately pinpointed the problem: the undisputed fact that between them the companies and the White union (whose leaders in those days can fairly be described as a 'wild' bunch, certainly more than just militant) had indulged in abuse of power, a reciprocal desire for revenge, and widespread greed.

On one score Morris felt White miners were entitled to sympathy:

'. . . were we (the non-mining community) in a situation where our position was threatened by this vast reservoir of African labour, which looms threateningly on the horizon, we might view the union's plight with greater understanding. Nevertheless, there is only one way in which Europeans can retain their position in the less-skilled grades of industry, and that is by continuing to outstrip the African in skill, integrity and efficiency. When we cease to do this we have no moral right to retain our vested interests.'

All the way through his sermon Morris was heckled by two union rowdies who refused to enter the church but made bawdy remarks from the doorway. They were, however, up against a master who had learned how to deal with hecklers on a soap box in the open air at Manchester. He had little difficulty in turning their interruptions to his own advantage, though the more traditional members of the congregation left the church thin-lipped and shocked, blaming their minister as much as the hecklers for allowing the House of God to be turned into a verbal boxing ring. Morris loved it, and over a cup of tea in the church hall afterwards continued the argument with his adversaries and some of the union men far into the night.

Other miners were not so disposed to engage in good natured badinage with the Fighting Parson. The Executive of the European Mine Workers' Union sent a demand to the Governor, Sir Arthur Benson, that Morris should be deported for 'fermenting industrial unrest' – a richly ironic viewpoint from a group of men who had paralysed the copper mines for over two months. The copper companies contented themselves with a formal statement to the Press repudiating Morris's claim that their withstanding of the union's demands was motivated by the desire for revenge.

The most costly strike in Northern Rhodesia's history petered out shortly afterwards. It would be too much to claim that Morris was solely responsible for creating a climate that made a settlement possible. But there is no doubt that his lucid analysis of the root causes of the trouble helped to bring to bear the pressure of public opinion upon the real issues. It was an outstanding demonstration of the power of a preacher (albeit in this case one with expert knowledge) to cut down through technicalities and express moral judgement with a logic impossible for all but the most bigoted to resist.

Whatever might be thought of its minister, Chingola Free Church was where the action was. Week by week the public flocked to church, curious, half-fearful or expectant, to hear what amounted to a forcefully expressed moral commentary on affairs of the day.

Municipal Councils, Mining Companies, White trade unions – Colin Morris was amassing a formidable array of enemies, though the man in the street (or pew) whilst aghast at the Fighting Parson's temerity, privately enjoyed the discomfiture of these Super-Powers which had hitherto been virtually beyond criticism. And possibly there was a half-deliberate tactic in Morris's peppering every target in sight. At least, this much was hinted at by the late Ian Hess, when Editor of the *Central African Examiner*. In an article he compared the unhappy fate of the Rev. Whitfield Foy in Salisbury, Southern Rhodesia, who was kicked out of his pulpit, and of the country, for his courageous defence of Black rights with Morris's extraordinary survival capacity, and asked 'Why does Morris survive whilst Foy goes under?' Hess wrote:

'Foy's controversial stand has been solely directed to political matters. Morris on the other hand has attacked virtually everything and everybody in sight: the copper companies (for closing Bancroft Mine); the European Mineworkers' Union (for abuse of power); the Government (for detaining political prisoners without trial); the community (for 'cowboy' driving, crass materialism and the Lord knows what else). Hence, by simple statistics, no matter whom Morris happens to be attacking, he is bound to have a section of the community behind him . . .'

It would be quite untrue to suggest that Morris's pulpit ministry was exclusively taken up in Jousting With Author-

43

ity. The routine work of the parish went on, much as anywhere else in Christendom – the ritual life-cycle symbolised by baptisms, weddings and funerals, the committees and women's meetings, the attention to people's personal problems. Though those who only knew of Morris through newspaper headlines could be forgiven for imagining that every Sunday his congregation were treated to a diatribe on some controversial issue, in fact the overwhelming majority of his pulpit work was orthodox, if rather vivid, preaching. One of his early books, *Out of Africa's Crucible*, was a volume of sermons he contributed to Lutterworth's *Preaching for Today* series. Of the twelve sermons it contains, four are concerned with what might be loosely described as social issues, the other eight with central Christian themes – probably a fair reflection of his routine preaching programme.

Casual visitors to his church and congregations in churches where he was a visiting preacher often went away disappointed not to have been given ammunition for some scandalised gossiping in the coming week. Merfyn Temple, fellow Methodist missionary and Morris's comrade in arms in the African freedom struggle, in a shrewd appraisal of Colin Morris he made in 1960 wrote:

'Many parsons and Church leaders baulk at letting Colin Morris loose on their congregations for fear of the repercussions. Their fears are needless since he makes it a rule never, unless invited to do so, to deal with highly controversial subjects from other ministers' pulpits. Hence congregations who do not know him and who go to hear him prepared to be outraged by what he says suffer almost from a sense of anti-climax when they are treated to a sermon, blameless in its orthodoxy . . .'[1]

Even at the height of the freedom struggle, one mistake Morris did not make was to become a 'one subject' preacher, hammering a single issue week in and week out. Around this period, addressing students at Mindolo Theological College on 'Preaching for our Time', he offered these

[1] K. Kaunda, *Black Government*, U.S.C.L., 1960, p. 40.

trainee-ministers some of the fruits of his hard experience and warned them:

'Do not become obsessionists, compressing the range of the Gospel into a single insight, however valid, on Race or Pacificism or Communism or anything else. Your congregation is not a pressure group organized to fight a single evil, however pervasive. It consists of people who need all the truth of God you can give them to get them through the week . . .

'Of course, your congregation must be challenged to lift their gaze beyond the horizon of their own front doors or the boundaries of their town. And this means confronting them with great issues they have never squarely faced or would rather avoid. But only those who have encountered the fulness of Jesus as Creator, Redeemer, and Lord have either the right or the knowledge to take their stand in the world for His Lordship over its manifold activities . . .

'. . . and, above all, when you tackle a controversial subject the infallible rule is: throw the Book at them! Make certain your argument is squarely based on Scripture. Then you can confidently take on the whole world if need be. For you are forcing those who resist you to argue not with you but against God's Word . . .'

This last suggestion was a tactic that Morris was afterwards to use with devastating effect, though there would be no shortage of devout churchmen to claim that his arguments supporting the social equality and political rights of Africans were based on highly individualistic interpretations of the Bible. Indeed, did not a whole Church, which yielded to no one in all the world for its reverence for Scripture, the Dutch Reformed Church, also base *its* case for *apartheid* and the denial of political rights to Africans on Biblical texts? Morris was on marshy ground here; not that an insecure footing ever worried him. With that sublime self-confidence his friends called faith and his enemies arrogance he never hesitated to plough his way forward, sometimes sinking deeper and deeper into the mire until he disappeared from sight when the cause he was supporting was ill-chosen. But he was more often right than wrong. His predictions had an uncanny way of being confirmed by events. As Canon George Hewitt, a pioneer Anglican missionary in Central Africa said of him: 'However outrageous Colin Morris's statements appear, it is always dangerous to argue; he is invariably proved right!'

Yet Morris proved that the vindicated prophet can expect little honour, either in his own country or anywhere else. As his notoriety grew, things were laid at his door for which he had not the slightest responsibility. If a report appeared in the Press that an African had attacked a European underground in one of the mines, his daily load of anonymous letters would greatly increase, all claiming (in varying degrees of illiteracy) that it was his doing. He was undermining law and order by his speeches and encouraging Africans to get out of hand. One incident Morris recalls with some amusement (now!) concerns a Sunday morning in his vestry when he was complaining to Maurice ffoulkes, his acting Church secretary, about the sheer illogicality of much of the abuse being heaped upon him. 'Don't worry, Colin!' chortled Maurice, the most unflappable of men, 'They'll be blaming you for the weather next!' Two mornings later, there appeared in the letter column of the *Northern News* a diatribe from a Pentecostalist pastor who drew attention to unseasonable rains that were disrupting the country's dry season and pointed out that according to Mark 13 the arrival of Antichrist on the scene produced pronounced meteorological consequences! Very funny, no doubt. But as he got tireder and his nerves began to fray, Morris found it harder to see such jokes.

He was rapidly becoming a ready-made scapegoat on which Whites with uneasy consciences could project their guilt – which they did with increasing ferocity. And in time he ceased the profitless exercise of attempting to answer publicly the crazy arguments of detractors who could think only with their blood.

5

It is not only what a man says, or even how he says it, that can stir things up. There are some personalities about whom people's feelings tend to polarize so sharply that the effect of their controversial speeches and actions is magnified. Because Colin Morris evokes extreme reactions of adulation or detestation, it is necessary to stop the projector, as it were, and get a close-up of the man behind the headlines so that the turbulent years that follow are more explicable.

This bane of die-hard Whites in Africa is a chunky man, with something of the pugilist about the set of his jaw and the solidity of his nose. The only indication of sensitivity is in his elegant hands which trace patterns in the air whilst he talks. He is never still. Foot-tapping, hand-waving, head-weaving; he is always in movement, radiating an almost frightening energy. When speaking in public, he talks with his whole body. He is not an elegant orator with studied gestures and delicately pronounced sentences. He pours forth torrents of words with a punch that leaves his hearers feeling bruised. One of his most valuable assets is a phenomenal memory. He delivers long speeches, larded with facts, statistics, and technical terms without notes whilst his eyes dart around his audience constantly as though daring them to relax their concentration for an instant.

Of his mastery of the spoken word even his bitterest enemies testify with reluctant admiration. He has been described by the *Central African Examiner* as 'the finest natural orator in Central Africa' – no mean compliment coming from an area that numbers men of the calibre of Sir Roy Welensky and Mr Garfield Todd amongst its public

47

performers. At times it has been the sheer power of his speaking that has enabled him to put across ideas so abhorrent to hostile audiences that he would probably have been lynched had he not hypnotized them into attention. But his very love for words can be a drawback. Some of his cleverest and most cutting aphorisms are directed not by personal spite against their target but rather as an exercise in word-spinning. One cannot, however, expect the unfortunate victim to know this, and personal relationships have sometimes suffered as a result.

Morris looks and is tough; it is not difficult to believe that he was once a Marine commando. He has the physical courage to plead unpopular causes before jeering crowds and the moral courage to chart a lonely course running counter to all that a White settler community believed in and was prepared to fight for. But he lacks the less dramatic courage to accept the burden of dull routine, to slog away at mundane but necessary tasks in a minister's life. He has an almost pathological aversion to writing letters, and spends pounds on telephone calls and telegrams rendered necessary by his dilatoriness with his correspondence.

He is a man who thrives on crises. When things are not on the boil and he has no fight on his hands, the fires of his personality are damped down and he drags around, picking at his work in desultory fashion, seizing any excuse to avoid tackling correspondence or make routine pastoral calls. A reluctant committee man, he used to be an inveterate late arriver and early departer, though it is widely conceded that once he has bent his mind to any matter on the agenda he has a keen analytical sense that cuts through irrelevancies and uncovers the guts of the issue. As President of the United Church of Zambia he is often required to preside at committees, and one colleague who has worked with him closely described him as having a gift for sitting through a discussion, apparently occupying himself with something quite different, and then suddenly intervening, giving a masterly summary of the trend of the discussion and phrasing an extempore resolution or minute that expresses the

48

committee's mind. But there is no doubt that this lone wolf finds committee work a special kind of martyrdom.

When things are quiet and his talents and energy are not harnessed to some important issue, Morris tends to be moody, introspective and not above taking refuge in a form of hypochondria his close friends easily recognise and generally indulge, making suitable sympathetic noises as he complains of ill-defined distempers that are rarely detected in medical examinations. He returned from a three-week visit to Vietnam at the height of the 1968 Tet Offensive in which he was exposed to considerable danger and had eaten and slept infrequently, looking the epitome of rude health; yet he will stagger in from some ecclesiastical conference grey-faced, haggard, protesting utter fatigue. His saving grace is that he has sufficient self-insight to recognise and laugh ruefully at this particular quirk.

Exasperated colleagues who do not understand how he ticks can be forgiven for finding his happy disregard for routine duties infuriating and labelling him irresponsible. However, having seen him unleash phenomenal physical and nervous energy in crisis situations, they tend to become more tolerant.

He is a law unto himself – a privileged status, some would argue, that he has earned by his contribution to the life of both Church and nation in Africa. Yet some of his keenest admirers wish that the energy and ability which he prodigally dispenses in all directions could be channelled by greater discipline into the central area of the work of the ministry. But had the 'cobbler stuck to his last' and minded his own business instead of concerning himself with social, industrial and political matters, the story of Zambia might have been very different. Certainly, thousands of Africans and Asians have cause to be grateful for this restless, probing man, who poked around in some of the murkiest corners of society and screamed to high heaven about what he saw.

Morris has a keen sense of the ridiculous and can give an impression of cheapening things which deep inside he values. On his study wall is a framed parchment, a warrant signed by President Kenneth Kaunda, appointing him to the Companion Order of Freedom for his 'exalted services in the cause of Zambia's Independence'. Beneath it, on his radio-gram, stands a little porcelain man, the epitome of pomposity, holding a notice that reads 'When you're as GREAT as I am, it's hard to be HUMBLE!' He is very proud of Zambia's official recognition of his services, but it must all be shrugged off with a somewhat cynical humour. Character-istically, he brags shamelessly about small things and yet is so self-deprecatory about some of the really important things he has done that it rings of a mock humility which is a form of affectation. But underneath the perpetual firework display of temperament, he *is* a humble man, receiving praise with an astonished naivety. Having been subjected to constant vilification he tends to look for ulterior motives in expressions of approval except from people whose judge-ment he has learned to trust.

He is a noisy man with a rich vein of vulgarity running through his character. He likes his entertainment moronic, his comedy slapstick and his novels earthy. His booming laugh in a cinema can drown the film's sound-track and bring down on his head hissed complaints from his neigh-bours. He has still not lived down the occasion he fell asleep in a performance of Mendelssohn's *Elijah* given by the local Choral Society, which included some members of his church choir. His loud snores shocked the culture-conscious members of the local community almost as much as the grunt of approval with which he came awake when Jezebel, played by the town's former Beauty Queen, came on-stage.

For all Morris's earthiness, there is a curious streak of puritanism in him. His extreme unclerical behaviour often tempts men of the world to treat him like one of the boys, and regale him with smutty stories. The punchline trails off as they find themselves looking into two granite-hard eyes in a set face. For him there is a world of difference between vulgarity and obscenity and those who cross the line are horrified to find him reacting like a Victorian bishop.

His taste in music is severely classical. He works always

against a background of a blaring radiogram booming forth Bach and Brahms – the noise made a bedlam by the barking of his two dogs, a Labrador and an Alsatian who, in true Morris tradition, have never been taught to keep quiet. His study is an eye-stinging, smoke-filled den in which he paces up and down like a caged lion. His books are always dictated; he hasn't the patience to sit for hours at a type-writer hammering away at chapter after chapter. He dictates at lightning speed to his secretary who is expected to catch every word he utters with a pipe clenched between his teeth; to spell, punctuate and paragraph as she goes along, and endure torrents of scathing abuse if she misses a word or looks up a spelling in the dictionary. Utterly impervious to the storm raging around her, she types stolidly on, indis-pensable not only by virtue of efficiency but also because the average secretary would soon retire with a nervous break-down brought on by working conditions unknown in Bri-tain since the passing of the Factory Act.

Only when Morris is dealing with people in real distress does his mad dash through life come to a halt. Then the phone is taken off its cradle, the radiogram is silent, and he has all the time in the world. The unchurched take their troubles to him because he is unshockable and they know that he will not fob them off with sentimental claptrap. He cuts through their confusion with a mind like a lance, helps them to face the truth, and themselves, sums up the alterna-tive courses of action open to them, and if asked, will tell them what he would do in their place. But the decision is always theirs. He never makes the mistake of becoming a crutch for the lazy-minded or weak-willed. He will do any-thing for them – his time, thought and restless energy are unconditionally at their disposal – he will do anything except allow them to take refuge in self-delusion. They will get the truth, unvarnished and straight from the shoulder. If they are willing to receive it, they get more – an infusion of some of his own great strength. But God help those who scurry to him with their petty jealousies or foolish complaints! His Church members long ago learned not to bother him with trivialities. In one of his early sermons he spelled out his pastoral attitude in typically vivid language. He said: 'I have no intention of playing nursemaid to Church members who will not grow up. If you are looking for a minister who will wipe your little noses and pat your bottoms, then you had better take your membership elsewhere. If you are anxious or troubled or lonely, then I'll be on your doorstep day or night. But so long as things go well for you, you must be prepared to take second place to those who need help.'

To see him at his best as a minister one must observe him dealing with the bereaved or at the bedside of a dying patient. The banter and bounciness vanish and a quality of gentleness few suspect him of having is paramount. At such times he is neither orator, controversialist nor prophet, but simply a man of shining faith. Certainly none of those who have found him a tower of strength in their darkest hours will give credence to the charges that he is merely a pulpit stunt-merchant or a politician sheltering in a priest's garb. They *know* what it means to be ministered to.

In the procession of the world's casualties who find their way to his door are not infrequently some of his bitterest detractors who have reviled him publicly and sworn never to set foot in his church. One, a senior official of Nchanga Mine, confessed, 'I've hated that man for years. In a sense I still do for what he has done to hustle this country into Black rule long before it is ready. But once when I was in the most desperate trouble and had a terrible decision to make, I was at my wits' end drinking more and more heavily as I tried to blot out my problem. Somehow or other I found myself on his doorstep, God knows how I got there! He knew who I was, all right, and what I thought of him. But he spent half the night thinking through my problem for me. He got me through the worst patch of my life. He didn't try to talk me into his Church or get me to change my attitude towards him. That night has never been mentioned since. Six months after, I was one of those who signed a petition demanding his deportation. And I think I was right. But I'll say this: he's a hell of a *big* man, that one.'

Writing in 1960, Merfyn Temple shrewdly describes Morris's love-hate relationship with the Church and his ministerial colleagues:

'In ecclesiastical circles, Morris is respected but not greatly loved by many of his brethren. Some senior ministers speak openly of him as a highly dangerous man. Nor can it be claimed that Morris goes out of his way to win their confidence. At a recent World Council of Churches Conference, he horrified distinguished Church leaders by declaring at a public meeting "There are too many women, of both sexes, running the modern Church."

'He is constantly enraging Church administrators with his scathing references to "ecclesiastical bureaucracy" and "death by a thousand committees." "The Church," he has commented, "has solved the problem of perpetual motion. It consists of an endless multiplicity of committees that exist by devouring each other's minutes." When challenged with his negative attitude to administrative matters he snapped: "When modern scholarship uncovers the fact that there was originally a Balance Sheet attached to the Book of the Acts of the Apostles, then I'll admit that this sort of thing is a worthwhile expenditure of energy ..."

'As with many of his utterances, there is sufficient truth in statements like these for them to be hurtful, and enough exaggeration to enrage hard-pressed administrators who want to help him all they can, and whose very efficiency allows him the freedom to be a prophet. He himself admits that he is not a good colleague or easy to work with. He does not seek willingly the company of his fellow ministers. Supremely confident of the rightness of the policy he has adopted, he can be less than charitable about the less spectacular work which others are doing. This lack of confidence in his brethren, it could be argued, stems from his bitter experiences. Few of them sprang to his defence at the time when public opinion was united against him. That period of his ministry has left its scars on him, and one of them is this lack of trust in his fellow ministers . . .'[1]

That was in 1960. In succeeding years, having been elected, to everyone's surprise and especially his own, to high office in two Union Churches, he has gained a wide reputation as a Church statesman. Possibly his political experience has reconciled him to the inevitability of committee work and administration. Though he shares a widespread disillusionment about the effectiveness of the organized Church with many other younger ministers, politics has taught him that power must be structured; it cannot exist as an abstraction, and this makes religious institutions necessary.

No profile of Colin Morris could pretend to be balanced without reference to the close-knit circle of friends who have supported him through thick and thin. They have often paid the price in social ostracism and loss of friends for defending and protecting him. Without them he would be utterly lost; they are his family, to whom he returns with great joy after his travels around the world. In their homes alone, three or four at most, does he feel able to be truly himself, let his hair down, work out his accumulated tension, and relax. Though these few stalwarts love and admire him they are in no sense sycophants. They are ruthless in keeping him up to the mark in important things and he can put *nothing* over on them. His torrents of eloquence are utterly wasted on them; his dramatic performances greeted with hoots of derision. A large share of the credit for Morris's achievements is due to them; not that, with his abhorrence of showing emotion, he is ever likely to tell them so – though he did dedicate his account of the racial struggle *The Hour After Midnight* to them 'in deep gratitude for unswerving loyalty and the forgiving spirit of true friendship'. And in that same book, commenting on a report in a London newspaper that 'the two most strategic pulpits in Southern Africa are those of St Mary's Cathedral, Johannesburg, bastion of Bishop Ambrose Reeves, and the Chingola Free Church',

[1]Ibid, p. 37.

he added: 'If there is any truth in this claim as far as the Chingola Free Church is concerned, then it should be understood that the credit is almost entirely due to a small embattled group of lay people who fought and won the battle in a thousand encounters with friends and acquaintances throughout the community . . . I merely sounded the trumpet; they did the fighting.'

6

So COLIN MORRIS was an explosive personality in an explosive situation. There are men who might have said the things he did and evoked only a sad head-shake of regret; Morris called out the demented hate of a whole community, as much as anything because he was the man he was. His very fluency and self-confidence fanned the flames. It is possible to envisage a minister humming and hawing his way through some tentative opinions on the subject of Race and getting away with a mild rebuke and the odd sneer. But Morris spoke (and speaks) with a degree of finality that makes what he says sound as though it was handed down to him personally from Mount Sinai that very morning. It was as though he had announced that the earth was round to a fourteenth century congress of flat-earthers, and did so with a degree of assurance that implied that no one in his right mind could possibly think otherwise.

Why did the man who pleaded for a cautious gradualism in the 1957 Methodist Synod blast the whole issue wide open and blow his congregation sky-high six months later? Possibly he was taking unpalatable doses of the medicine he handed out to his pastoral cases, absolute honesty, and saw that he had been deluding himself and his congregation with his belief in gradualism; that people's attitudes on an issue as violent as Race could not be corrected by a mild dose of mental physiotherapy but only by major surgery. The most likely reason, however, was that he was for the first time making contact with that elusive, and, to European minds, sinister group of Africans who were stirring up their people to revolt against inhuman living conditions and political disability. These men, the early freedom-fighters of Northern Rhodesia, went about by day performing menial and innocuous jobs as teachers or clerks, but at night they planned and organized and dreamt of the day when British colonial rule would be overthrown and Black men rule their own land – men like Kenneth Kaunda, Harry Nkumbula, Simon Kapwepwe, Sikota Wina.

It was Sikota Wina who first sought out the controversial missionary in order to get an interview for the *Nchanga Drum* – a newspaper run for African mineworkers of which Wina was chief (and only) reporter. Wina was quite unlike any other African Morris had met in his first year in Northern Rhodesia. Articulate, intense, the tall Lozi of his own age, whose history had already been a stormy one, fascinated Morris, and a routine news interview was transformed into a profound dialogue in which the Fighting Parson faced for the first time the possibility that he had been fighting for the wrong things, or at least had been going into battle against minor evils whilst a major one stared him in the face.

Son of a former prime minister of Barotseland (an area at that time a British Protectorate within Northern Rhodesia, and today the Barotse Province of independent Zambia) Wina had been expelled from Fort Hare, an African university in South Africa, for taking part in a students' strike. Morris quickly perceived that within him there burned indignation and fierce pride of race – feelings honed to sharp bitterness by the kind of life he was having to lead through being deprived of his right to education. Wina had been forced to scale down his driving ambition and bend his considerable literary talent to writing smalltown newspaper items about over-filled dustbins and re-siting of bus stops in local streets.

He and Morris were drawn to each other, partly because of their mutually rebellious natures, partly because they felt so at ease in each other's company. Unlike most of the educated Africans Morris had met in the territory up to that time, Wina did not, in his dealings with Europeans, veer unpredictably between abject servility and overweening

57

arrogance in the I'm As Good As Any White Man sense. Completely without self-consciousness in a European environment, his demeanour defied Morris or anyone else to treat him with other than absolute equality.

Wina became a frequent visitor to the manse, providing for Morris the first undistorted glimpse of the facts of life on the other side of the colour barrier. The two were able to discuss the most explosive subjects frankly and without heat. Wina, unlike most Africans, never retired hurt when a shaft struck home about the shortcomings of his own kind.

Nor did he allow politeness to deter him from exposing the hypocrisies and thoughtless cruelties of Europeans in their dealings with other races.

Sikota Wina gave Morris a political education simply by posing to him unanswerable questions. For example: what was the logic or justice in a state of affairs where he and his brother Arthur, at that time the highest-ranking African in the territorial education service, could fly half way round the world to America and back receiving courtesy and consideration every mile of the journey, only to be humiliated and insulted when they returned to their homeland?

Morris could not tell him. The most he could do was pass these questions on to European friends. How do you explain to a man like Wina why a European child addresses him as 'Boy'? Why was he thrown out of an airport bar when he was simply trying to buy some cigarettes? Why must he use a separate entrance to the post office from Whites who had neither his education nor his culture? The replies were unvarying. It was tough on people like Wina and his very capable brother, but to lower the barriers for the mere handful of educated Africans would be to let in the whole backward horde. Wina and his like would just have to mark time until their more primitive brothers caught up with them.

Morris could only retire in frustration. It was obvious that Europeans saw Africans, whatever their achievements, as nothing more than walking extensions of a shovel or dishcloth. Time and again he was reminded: 'Scratch a Black B.A. and you will uncover a cannibal.'

After leaving the *Drum*, Wina edited an independent African newspaper before becoming an active official of the Zambia African Congress, the country's first organized indigenous political party. Congress was banned in 1959 and Wina was among those arrested in a midnight police swoop. He was rusticated to a remote rural village, there to brood upon his grievances.

When next Morris met him, they were almost strangers. Wina had left behind him in detention camp his gentle humour and urbane manner. He was now a hard, unrelenting nationalist, complete with toga and Nkrumah-type haircut, whose vocabulary seemed limited to the cry 'We demand self-government'. He and Morris found little to say to each other: the common ground between them had been devastated by Wina's experience. All that remained was a rather taut, reserved, mutual respect. But it can be recorded that the passage of time saw a re-blossoming of their early friendship. But by then Morris's friend was better known as the Honorable Sikota Wina, Minister of Local Government in the government of the Republic of Zambia.

It was through Wina that Morris met another African who had considerable impact upon him, a shrewd and jolly trade union leader named Lawrence Katilungu – a man with an incredible knack for holding the confidence of both Africans and Europeans in the mining world.

Katilungu's greatest gift was probably his uncanny understanding of European psychology, so there is little doubt he soon had the Fighting Parson taped. The barely-educated unionist and the Oxford graduate got on well together because of their common interest in the industrial life of the country and because, like Wina, Katilungu called a spade a spade when it came to criticizing the shortcomings of people, whether Black or White.

Katilungu was leader of the African Mineworkers' Union whose 40,000 members comprised the biggest organized local labour force in the country. He and Morris spent hours talking over the problems of African advancement and job discrimination. Not infrequently Katilungu's negotiating brief in some dispute with the mining companies would betray evidence of Morris's impeccable English style and expert knowledge of labour relations.

Europeans and Africans mourned when Katilungu was killed in a car crash. Indeed, the White miners' union set up a trust fund for his widow and children to which £4,000 was subscribed.

Only one hour before his death Katilungu concluded an interview with the author for an article destined for the American magazine *Newsweek*. 'One day soon I will enter the political arena . . . I am confident I can get both Black and White support and set the stage for Africa's first truly multi-racial society . . .' That prediction was printed in *Newsweek* as his obituary.

'Through constant discussion with Africans of this calibre my thinking underwent a radical change,' says Morris. 'The arguments of my European friends began to weigh less and less with me as it became clear how remote they were from any sustained contact with articulate Africans, and as I was privileged to share the hopes and fears of a group of men whom anyone would have been proud to hail as friends. Even more than their burning sense of grievance their charitableness and freedom from bitterness impressed me. They rejected absolutely the view that Europeans are innately bad, recognizing that the social set-up allowed them little latitude to be anything else.'

In the public announcements column of the *Nchanga Weekly* towards the end of March, 1958, there appeared a Church notice to the effect that on three Sunday evenings in Lent the Minister of the Free Church would preach three sermons on the subject 'Christianity and Race', questions invited and a cup of tea thrown in. By the end of the third sermon his congregation had been scattered to the four winds, his brand new church was sunk deep in debt, and he was a national figure – of abuse! 'The Fighting Parson has taken a wrong turn,' sadly commented a *Northern News* leader, it apparently having slipped the mind of the editor that only months before he had been pleading for 'the voice of religion to be heard loud and clear in the councils of the land.' 'We've got a Huddleston, too!' exalted the irrepressible *African Times*.

'Thank God he's taken the plunge at last!' said one of Morris's friends, watching him agonizing over the inexorable progression of his thinking towards a position that must put him at odds with the bulk of his congregation and make him an outcast from the White community. With a somewhat untypical caution, Morris decided in tackling his subject to avoid the more contentious political aspects of the racial struggle and keep strictly to what the Bible had to say about the unity of all men and its practical consequences – 'Throw the Book at 'em!' he had advised the Mindolo theological students. He had tactfully refrained from warning them about what was likely to be thrown back in retaliation.

In retrospect, a reading of those three sermons, published shortly after delivery by Lutterworth Press under the title *Anything But This!*, shows them to have been strongly biblical in emphasis, expressing views of unimpeachable orthodoxy on the subject of Race, enlivened by the odd typical Morrisism. In 1968, it is difficult to understand what all the fuss was about. Ten years before, his words were sparks amid the stubble. He revealed himself as a traitor in the camp. As world opinion blew cold upon the White Settlers of Africa, and the rising tide of nationalism lapped at the walls of their fortress, from within came a cry from one of their own kind that shattered their unity and denied them even the consolations of religion in a tough time. Yet for once the Fighting Parson wasn't looking for a fight, but pleading for understanding. He didn't get it. The very violence of the reaction to his sermons drove him further and deeper into the racial struggle. His pact of mutual non-aggression with his community on the subject of Race was broken for ever.

A record congregation attended the first of the three services. People *were* worried about the rising racial tension on the Copperbelt; maybe they were hoping that their attitudes would be justified rather than challenged. After all, the Fighting Parson, whatever his intemperateness on other issues, had hitherto been the model of discretion on this one. Being essentially decent people, they were even prepared for a little gentle prodding, a few practical suggestions about racial co-operation, some judicious balancing of the rival claims of Black and White. Instead, a vigorously wielded sledge-hammer was applied to the very structure of their society. Not only had they to contend with an unsympathetic British Government and the growing animosity of African nationalists, but apparently God was against them as well!

Morris began his sermon with typical candour, confessing the extent to which he had misled his people and deluded himself by the comforting and reassuring word 'gradually'. 'Give all the time in the world I would seek to be a gradualist, but we haven't got all the time in the world, the speed at which the two races are moving towards collision point is increasing, the climate of feeling is deteriorating. Both our races are beginning to think with their blood.' Announcing his text as 'My House shall be a House of Prayer for all nations', he added, 'I know of no way to make that verse read 'A House of Prayer for all nations – except the Africans.'

Declaring any form of discrimination, racial or otherwise, to be contrary to the Will of God, and an affront to all that Christ taught, Morris asked: 'Where do we stand in the Church?'

'We are witnesses of a situation in which thousands of God's children are suffering obvious injustice. And our course of action should be clear; for what is wrong from the standpoint of common justice can never be right from the standpoint of Christian ethics. Yet is it not a fact that our pronouncements lack conviction because in some cases our own hands are not clean? Our trumpet gives forth uncertain sound because the attitudes we know we should deplore in the community are also represented in the Church. Do we in the Church exhibit in our worship the unity in Christ which should transcend all racial barriers? When the community looks towards us are they judged by us as they see demonstrated in practice the fact that in Christ, and in the place where His people meet "there is neither Jew nor Greek, bond nor free, male or female"? Or are they not in a position to say "Despite all their pious pronouncements, when we get down to brass tacks, they are with us"? To what extent are we guilty of racial discrimination before the very altar of God? Only you personally can answer that question. Would you personally welcome an African as he took his place beside you in worship and knelt beside you in prayer? Would you personally hear gladly the Word of God from the lips of my African colleague and receive humbly from his hands the Body and Blood of Our Lord? If we cannot truly answer "Yes!" to these and similar questions, then we stand judged of God, for we are allowing our human prejudices to hold sway in the place where the Will of Christ should rule supreme.'[1]

At this point in Morris's peroration two people in the front pew stood up, deposited their hymn books firmly on their seats, pushed past their neighbours and stalked out of the church, slamming the door behind them with a crash that rattled the windows. Morris paused in mid-sentence, gulped, then went on with his exposition. 'If more church-goers were to express their opinions so forcefully about the parson's sermons no doubt the quality of preaching would improve, but it's a hell of a shock the first time it happens!' he afterwards recalled.

The handshakes of the congregation as they filed out after the service were noticeably less cordial than usual. Morris held a post mortem with one or two of his Church Council members. 'Well, Colin, you gave it to 'em hot and strong,' said one, 'but you said what you believed, and they'll respect you for it.' Others were not so sure, 'Next Sunday will tell; let's see how many of them come back for more!' Anyone in the community who hadn't heard about the ser-

'Morris, *Anything But This!* Lutterworth, 1958, p. 13.

mon was treated to a highly stylised version in the *Northern News* of the following morning:

CHURCH FINISHED UNLESS IT BANS
DISCRIMINATION SAYS FIGHTING PARSON

ran the headline.

Morris spent much of the ensuing week taking stock of the situation. If he had hoped for any marked degree of support from his clerical brethren he was quickly disabused by a letter which appeared in the press, signed by a local priest and pleading with the public not to judge the whole Church by Colin Morris. And the chairlady of the women's meeting of the local Gospel Hall stopped him in the street and assured him that he had been the subject of a long prayer session that morning. The fervent ladies had beseeched the Almighty, not to give him the courage of his convictions, but to show him the error of his ways!

'Next Sunday will tell!' . . . and it did. Morris's words echoed hollowly around a three-parts empty church. His second sermon cut deeper into the raw nerve of the community than his first. It was one thing to attack the colour bar in the Church; after all, that affected only a minority of people, and if they were happy to share their pews with 'kaffirs' it was their own business. But this time he threw down the gauntlet at the community as a whole by attacking the 'tissue of lies masquerading as biological and theological doctrines of the superiority of the White race, often imported from South Africa.' Since probably seventy-five per cent of Copperbelt Whites were of South African origin, he could hardly have expected a warm reception to be accorded to his sermon. Nobody walked out of the church on this occasion but a young, intelligent couple whose friendship he had valued and whose support he counted on shook him sadly by the hand after the service and announced, 'You will never see us in this church again!' Their reaction was typical of many who did not even bother to tell him that they were cutting themselves off from the church. Friendship can survive many blows, but the racial question touched life at so many points in Central Africa that people who could not see

64

eye to eye on it had precious little left upon which to base friendly relations.

That second week brought the first of the anonymous letters, the scurrilous telephone calls, the deliberate snubs in the street that were to become a part of Morris's life for years. Easter Day dawned, as usual gloriously sunny, but the sense of anticipation with which the Christian greets the great festival of the Church was dimmed for Morris by the self-evident fact that far from the usual thronging congregation, many of whom paid their annual visit to church on that day, he was likely to balance the record numbers of recent years with an all-time low. And so it proved. The note of Easter triumph in his voice was almost hysterical as he surveyed the rows of empty pews and, at the back of the church, the forlorn stacks of chairs normally necessary to squeeze the congregational overflow into every available inch of space. And to his disappointment was added resentment when one of his friends reported gloomily that every other church in the town had done record business. The congregation he had laboriously built up fled in all directions for the consolations of religion. It was a poignant demonstration of the strength of racial feeling that staunch Nonconformists who normally blanched with horror at the idea of kneeling, genuflecting, incense and all that, preferred to swallow the inbred religious prejudices of generations and worship where they could be sure the sermon subject would be 'religion' rather than endure another of Morris's tirades from the pulpit.

In succeeding weeks, Morris and his handful of loyal supporters took stock of the situation. The uproar did not die down but seemed to gain greater strength. The stone he had dropped into the placid pool in Chingola spread outwards in ripples of controversy that engulfed the entire Territory. Besides the anonymous filth he found in his mail were increasing numbers of letters from Women's Institutes and clubs of various kinds who had earlier asked him to address them, cancelling the arrangement. They were so sorry but they had got the date wrong and engaged another speaker, or their committee felt that it would be disturbing to the peace of the club if he were to appear before them. One service club in Mufulira, whose members were vigorous young men, sent a letter saying bluntly that they could not guarantee his safety. Or proprietors of the halls or restaurants in which such meetings were normally held, fearful of their property, had laid down the law and said 'No Colin Morris or the club must find another venue.' The reasons and excuses varied but the upshot was the same – the most popular speaker in the Territory couldn't find an audience to listen to him.

Loose newspaper reporting did not help. One newspaper resurrected a speech Morris had delivered months before at a Christian Council meeting in which, commenting on the fact that the works of Karl Marx were banned in Northern Rhodesia, he had roundly declared that if the Government wanted to prevent Africans from getting revolutionary ideas about their rights, it was the Bible that ought to be banned for, he added, 'Karl Marx was a bowler-hatted conservative compared with the Galilean Carpenter.' Hence, an explosive headline:

BAN THE BIBLE!
CRIES THE FIGHTING PARSON

and those who did not bother to read the story beneath the big black letters had their worst suspicions confirmed that Morris was a communist agitator in clerical dress who rated *Das Kapital* higher than the Word of God. The first of many petitions demanding his deportation began to circulate. Morris signed a copy outside Chingola's main store held out to him by a formidable housewife who obviously hadn't recognized him. It was an act of almost desperate bravado – his way of shrugging off with a grin and a ruefully told anecdote against himself his deep inner hurt. As he signed with a flourish, he noted with shock that amongst the other signatures were those of some of the most respected members of the community. He knew now that the storm would not blow over. He had delivered a sword-thrust that left a wound which would never completely heal. Nor has it. Ten years later there are Chingola Whites who speak of him with a long-nourished hatred that time has not abated.

Most painful of all was the effect upon his pastoral work. Hearing one night that the son of a family associated with his church for many years had been seriously injured in a car crash, he hurried down to the hospital to be informed by an embarrassed nursing sister that the boy's father had given strict instructions that Morris was not to see him, and that should his condition deteriorate the Anglican priest was to be called. Wedding invitations announcing that the venue of the Happy Event was to be the Chingola Free Church were hastily scrapped and new ones printed with another church substituted. Neither their babies for baptism, their young people for marriage nor their dead for burial would the community entrust to the traitor in their midst. For three months the only burials Morris conducted were those of two suicides, and only then because other Churches had stern rules about the disposal of the remains of those who had taken their own lives.

Everywhere people argued, over their beer in the Mine Club or their whisky in the golf house, down the mine, in the shops. Morris's supporters, heavily outnumbered, gave a good account of themselves, and accepted their share of ostracism and insult. This was the Church Militant with a vengeance! Reports of Morris's latest doings or utterances were savoured at morning bridge parties, afternoon teas or evening dinners. And what people didn't know, they invented. His racial views were attributed to his predilection for Black women and his political views to the fact that he was an agent of Moscow.

There were compensations for the odium heaped upon him by the White community. Morris realized with gratitude the strength and quality of his friends. He was not alone. His army might well be Lilliputian, but every soldier was a 'bonny fighter'. His tiny Sunday congregation might roll around like peas in a drum in the big church, but at least they were not merely formal churchgoers; every one was committed – they were those 'doers of the Word and not

67

hearers only' of whom Jesus talked. Raring for a fight, they spurred Morris on to tackle other aspects of the colour bar at times when he would gladly have crawled away to hide from the outcry. In succeeding months discrimination in local cafés, shops and industry were the subjects of scorching sermons. And once he had spoken, his church acted. Members who never before had met an African socially threw open their homes, they boycotted stores and cafés where Africans were badly treated. Two of his congregation, both teachers, started an unofficial school for Coloured children, who, being officially classified neither Black nor White, were debarred from attending both the schools in the European township and those in the African compounds. Morris began a violent agitation to have the town's only cinema opened to Asian citizens. He wrote letters to the Government, pestered MPs, and created such a furore that six months later the first self-conscious Asians were able to watch the exploits of Gary Cooper triumphing single-handed over another brand of Indian.

'It is human dignity that is at stake,' declared Morris in one sermon, 'and the Church has no option but to support the African and Asian people in their fight to assert their God-given humanity.' That was certainly a fancy way of describing the general mêlée he was causing throughout the community. But it was true. Beneath all the ferment and strife a frontier was slowly emerging, dividing those who stood for human dignity from those who, however unintentionally, were violating it. And possibly Morris's great offence in the eyes of many decent Whites was that he did not allow them to maintain any position of neutrality. They were forced to declare themselves. Echoing some words of George Macleod he thundered 'Those who sit on modern fences tend to get electrocuted.'

7

IF one compensation for the White hatred Morris was engendering was the support of loyal friends, another was the new sense of hope he was giving to Africans who had long since despaired of things ever changing. In his own words:

'Apparently the fact that I was secure in the detestation of Europeans was sufficient credential for the African people, the vast majority of whom had never met me or heard me speak. Soon, my mail box bulged with letters sent by Africans from all over Northern Rhodesia – some, grubby pencil-written and under-stamped, others impeccably typed and expressing in fluent English the most erudite views on every subject under the sun. I was deeply touched at the pathetic confidence many of my correspondents had in my ability to find them wives, get them out of police custody, guarantee bank loans and, as an invariable post-script, smash the Federation . . . These themes constantly recurred – their hatred of Federation, their fierce resentment of the colour bar and their joy that the Church appeared to be coming more articulate on behalf of the voiceless and voteless peoples of Central Africa . . .'

Colin Morris had, in fact, become a national hero amongst Africans. In their study of the growth of the Church in Northern Rhodesia, John Taylor and Dorothea Lehmann relate that whilst doing their research they were present at a meeting of the Luanshya branch of the African National Congress at which a proposal to boycott the country's churches was hotly debated. The matter was dispatched in one sentence by an official who declared 'Let us leave the Church of Colin Morris alone.'[1] And the authors go on to

[1]Taylor & Lehmann, *Christians of the Copperbelt*. S.C.M., 1961, p. 158.

relate another incident:

'My colleague (Dr Lehmann) experienced a similar reaction at Nchanga during our study in 1958. Whilst she was sitting in the yard of a house in the compound talking to a group of women two of the more radical Congress youths began to abuse the women, calling out "What does this White person want? Why do you talk to her?" Their shout quickly drew a hostile crowd. But at that point a third youth pressed through the crowd, crying, "Leave this European alone; do not stop her in her work. She is a friend of Colin Morris." Immediately the atmosphere cleared, the youths stayed to listen to the discussion and the crowd showed no sign of hostility when the women accompanied my colleague to her car.'

Dr Taylor goes on to ask:

'Why is it that Mr Morris should have won this unique reputation? He himself would certainly be the first to agree that he is not the only White minister in Northern Rhodesia to have "interfered" in politics . . . The explanation probably lies in the fact that in this situation of acute disillusionment, the only guarantee for Africans that a European is to be trusted is that he is prepared to forfeit the trust of the majority of Europeans. Only as European Christians are seen to suffer at the hands of their own people will African Christians become assured that they are so committed to their principles that they will not revert to type when the pressure comes . . .'[1]

Colin Morris would certainly agree that he was not the first White minister in Northern Rhodesia to take a stand for racial equality, and indeed, in his book *The End of the Missionary?* he catalogues a long series of statements and protests by missionaries and Church conferences, going back to 1923, on behalf of their African charges. But it is safe to say that no White minister in Central Africa before him dramatized the issue in such stark terms, went so far in his demands or publicized his views so widely in the press.

[1]Ibid. p. 158

He initiated a national debate in the newspaper correspondence columns that had letters pouring in upon their editors in hundreds, many of which were unprintable. For months on end, never a day went past without Morris being the subject of at least a couple of letters, mostly hostile, but occasionally expressing support. Comments John Taylor, 'The word "Parson" alone in the headlines was sufficient to indicate who was the subject of the article.' And when the papers were not carrying a report of one of his speeches or sermons, there would be an account of a public attack upon him by a Cabinet minister or a leader article chiding him for his intemperance. Morris was attracting more publicity than even the Federal Prime Minister, Sir Roy Welensky, himself no mean headline-getter.

It was all very exhilarating but the wear and tear on the Lancashireman's nerves was beginning to become apparent to his anxious friends. There was no respite from the clamour. The public saw to that. A group of copper miners formed a syndicate in which they took it in turns to phone him round the clock. A couple on night shift would phone him at intervals throughout the night, either putting down the phone when he answered or shouting obscenities; then a couple on day shift would continue the torment from five o'clock in the morning, and so it went on. And Morris dare not take refuge in removing his receiver in order to get some sleep. It was just possible that the hospital was trying to reach him, or a parishioner with an urgent problem. From time to time threats of physical violence reached such proportions that his friends insisted on escorting him when he went out at night to answer calls.

The Fighting Parson was thus, if not on the ropes, at least somewhat punch drunk when the biggest storm of all broke over him. It was something of a time bomb, the aftermath of one of his famous Lenten sermons on the Race issue. The three sermons had been published and the first copies reached the Federation. A sharp newspaper reporter leafing idly through a review copy noticed a couple of paragraphs that the press had apparently overlooked at the time of delivery. These paragraphs dealt with the most explosive aspect of the whole racial question – inter-marriage. If White settlers got heated at the prospect of having to meet Africans socially they became homicidal at the suggestion of any inter-marriage between the Races. 'Brother, I'm with you all the way,' commented Morris's outspoken Women's Guild chairlady when he mentioned that he was dealing with inter-marriage in the course of the sermons, 'but on that one I have a complete blank spot, so watch it!' Suitably warned, Morris chose his words with great care when he dealt with what he termed 'the revulsion that confounds logic as White Rhodesians succumb to the atavistic fear that stems from the dread of White purity being ravaged by Black savagery.' Then he went on:

'If you were to put me on the spot and ask me what I would advise my daughter if she announced her intention of marrying an African, I can only say that I would counsel her to extreme caution without actually forbidding the match. I would point out with due parental pomposity the desirability of marriage being based upon a kinship of interest and similarity of background. I would advise her to visit her prospective husband's parents and see where and how they live, and realize that she might possibly have to live under similar conditions. I would also point out the possible fate of any children of the match in the present climate of our society. If she remained adamant, I would do all in my power to ensure the success of the marriage and intensify my fight for the kind of society in which her children need not be victimised.'[1]

Nobody present in the church the day the sermon was delivered took more exception to his treatment of the fear of racial inter-marriage than anything else he said. But six months later, those five fatal words 'without actually forbidding the match' were to boomerang upon his head in a scalp-crawling headline in the *Sunday Mail*:

MY DAUGHTER COULD MARRY A NATIVE, SAYS FIGHTING PARSON

[1] C. Morris, *Anything But This!*, Lutterworth, 1958, p. 54

The Sunday morning the story appeared Morris did not see his newspaper until after the service, and so was puzzled by the air of tension that pervaded the congregation. 'This time you've gone too far!' snapped a member of his Church Council as he stalked through the church door, ignoring Morris's outstretched hand. Morris shook his head in bewilderment. He had preached a sermon of impeccable orthodoxy on the Parable of the Grain of Mustard Seed. Race, Africans, politics, none of the explosive ingredients of former controversies were mentioned in it. It was a strictly 'religious' sermon. Yet a Church Council member who had stuck it grimly through all his fiery utterances on the racial issue apparently baulked at a piece of biblical exposition. When he went back through to his vestry to disrobe, muttering to himself about the plain cussedness of these extraordinary Whites, Arthur Short silently handed him a copy of the newspaper with the headline blazoned across it. Beneath it was an extract from that part of his sermon, words and sentences taken out of context in order to give the reader the impression that Morris would regard the marriage to an African of his mythical daughter not with fatherly concern but with high delight.

For weeks the uproar convulsed the Territory. Abuse rained down upon Morris from every conceivable quarter. The Executive of the European Mineworkers' Union passed a unanimous resolution demanding his immediate deportation, failing which they would bring the mines to a standstill. Housewives' Leagues petitioned their MPs and the Governor asking for his removal in the interests of the safety of their daughters. In Luanshya a mob of youngsters publically burned copies of his book in the car park of the Mine Club. He had a curt note from the Federal Broadcasting Corporation informing him that he had been banned from the radio; he was no longer one of the panel of churchmen whose privilege it was to offer five minutes encapsulated religious inspiration to begin the day's broadcasting.

The furore was made worse by the fact that since the bookshops of the Federation were showing a marked reluctance to stock and sell the book, the African National Congress took over its distribution in the African townships. The *Northern News* carried a story to the effect that Congress had sold over five hundred copies in a single day. A statement from Samson Mukondo, Chairman of the Nchanga Branch of the Congress was quoted: 'This book is, in my opinion, the first serious contribution to the solution of the problem of race relationships that faces us all.' White settlers had no doubt what the essence of the solution was that Morris advocated – the creation of a coffee-coloured race!

Half-submerged beneath a mountain of abusive letters for publication in the *Northern News*, its Editor was forced to print a special statement pointing out that there were stringent legal penalties against the printing of obscene and blasphemous letters and that he was thus unable to use most of his daily mail-bag. But the ones that did appear provided a striking confirmation of Morris's own sermon comment that the subject of inter-marriage touched the rawest nerve of all. Wrote *Chingola Mother*:

'I wondered how long it would be before we experienced the repercussions of Colin Morris's shocking statement. Only the other day my teenage daughter was accosted in the street by an African boy who very politely told her that he was making up his mind whether or not to marry her...'

Wrote *Mother of Four*:

'It is no longer safe for our daughters to walk the streets without being leered at by some would-be Black rapist...'

And a Broken Hill matron expressed her indignation at the apathy of fathers:

'I notice that most of the letters bitterly resenting (and how rightly) the shocking ideas put forward by the Rev. Colin Morris, are written by mothers. How apathetic can the fathers get?'

The scurrilous phone calls and anonymous letters multiplied. Morris was hissed in the street and was greeted by an angry wave of foot-stamping when he went to the cinema.

Added to this was a campaign of petty persecution which, though more irritating than worrying, made it difficult for him to do his job – telephone engineers 'forgot' to fix his telephone when it went wrong; municipal employees failed to turn up to repair light or water breakdowns; his newspapers were not delivered; grocery orders were mislaid. A whole community made it abundantly clear that he was an outcast, a creature of nameless depravity, not fit for decent company. Numerous plans to have him tarred and feathered were hatched in various places, one of which might well have succeeded had it not been for his Alsatian bitch, Liz, who scattered a gang of young thugs that congregated outside his house. It became a sporting pastime for schoolboys to hurl stones on to the tin roof of his manse. Appeals to the police to curb them elicited a bored response that indicated clearly that in their view he deserved all he was getting, and more.

Morris haunted the homes of his close friends (possibly there were only a dozen homes in the entire community that would allow him across the threshold) pacing restlessly back and forth, debating with them and himself whether he had any right to subject the Chingola Free Church to the consequences of his words and actions. Every Church Council meeting was a doleful recital of resignations and falling finances. Letters were read out from long-standing supporters of the Church whose message amounted to 'either he goes or we go . . .' Finally, in a mood of black despair after a dismal Sunday in which the congregation reached an all-time low, Morris sought out his Church Secretary and offered his resignation. He had failed, utterly and abjectly, to gain the understanding of his people, to win their confidence or carry them with him. He had harmed the church and subjected his friends to impossible strains upon their loyalty. And deepest-seated of all was the fear that he might be making race relations worse rather than improving them.

As the Church Council debated his resignation, Morris paced up and down outside his vestry, listening to the buzz of voices and reviling himself for his stupidity in pitching into an issue that wiser ministers left well alone. Eventually, Arthur Short recalled and read out to him in an expressionless voice the terms of a resolution the Council had passed in the matter of his resignation. It 'expressed appreciation of the minister's courageous stand on the great issue of the day' and 'assured him of full support in the influential and helpful ministry being rendered in both church and community.'

Morris was overwhelmed. He knew what those few words would cost the Council, the pressures they would have to resist, the charges and misrepresentations that would be laid at their door. Most of all he was aware that some of the more conservative of them had grave reservations about the wisdom of what he was doing, and felt that he was pushing things along much faster than prudence decreed. But to a man (and woman) they endorsed the most precious liberty a minister possesses, that of speaking the truth as he sees it without fear or favour.

The firm handshakes and encouraging words of the Council members as they filed out of the meeting lifted Morris out of his black depression. His base was firm. The Church had spoken. He was not a publicity-loving individualist, lashing out in all directions with utter irresponsibility. Men and women of shrewd judgement and firm Christian belief had confirmed the rightness of his stand and, more, had resolved to back him in whatever future action, however controversial, he felt impelled to take. And for their part, they determined to give more and work harder to ensure that the doors of the church from which Colin Morris was speaking to Central Africa's conscience should remain open.

As time went on, the climate of the community slowly subsided from one of frenzied hate for Morris to one of quiet detestation. He went about his work, arguing and pleading endlessly, adding ones and twos to his congregation, taking the opportunity of winning over anyone with even a slightly open mind. But in the highly charged emotional atmosphere of Central Africa it was inevitable that crisis should succeed crisis. And Chingola Free Church found itself in the thick of the battle again in 1959 as a consequence of what became widely known as the Ibiam Incident.

Sir Francis Ibiam, a distinguished Nigerian doctor and Governor of Eastern Nigeria, was driving from Elizabethville in the Belgian Congo to Ndola in order to catch a plane to London. He decided to break his journey in Chingola for a cup of tea, and being accustomed to the more civilized racial attitudes of the West Coast walked into a café, sat down and gave his order to the astonished waiter. To his shock and indignation he was asked to leave. Apparently neither the accolade of knighthood nor membership of the Privy Council was sufficient guarantee that, being Black, he could conform to the civilized standards of behaviour of the teenage White youths, lounging around, playing the fruit machines and jeering at him.

Within twenty-four hours the incident was front page news in the Federation's newspapers and apologies descended upon Sir Francis from all directions. Sir Roy Welensky expressed regret on behalf of the people of the Federation, the Governor of Northern Rhodesia added his on behalf of the Territory, the Chingola Municipal Council made a grudging apology, hastening to defend the café proprietor by pointing out that he wasn't to know that Sir Francis was anyone other than an 'ordinary African'.

Morris was furious when the news of the incident reached him, and called an immediate meeting of his Church Council, who expressed 'shame and indignation' that their town had been so inhospitable, not only to a distinguished world figure but also, by implication, to its humblest African citizen who daily shared his fate. They sent a telegram to the Governor demanding legislation outlawing racial discrimination once and for all in public places. His anger unappeased, Morris cast about for some other way of confronting the apathetic people of Chingola with the enormity of what they had connived at by their support of the colour bar. In the end he obtained a nine-foot square board upon which he had painted in letters a foot high:

THIS CHURCH
IS
COLOUR BLIND

The board was erected on the boundary of the Church grounds facing a main road. The resultant angry hootings of passing motorists showed that it was being read – if not appreciated. During the night, someone got busy with a pot of black paint and the peace of Morris's Sabbath morn was shattered by the ringing of the telephone. It was one of his Council members, informing him that the board now read:

THIS CHURCH
IS
BLIND

Hastily recruiting Howarth Senogles, one of his more mechanically-minded Council members who had had the board made in the first place, Morris went up to the church and they got busy with a bottle of turpentine. He dashed into the pulpit, his cassock splattered with paint and smelling of turpentine, but the original message was there to confront his congregation.

The following morning the Town Engineer rang the Fighting Parson to inform him that the board contravened at least half a dozen of the town's by-laws and would have to be taken down. 'Not at all,' he concurred cheerfully, secretly relieved that he had a graceful face-saver, since it was clear he could not spend the rest of his life dashing backwards and forwards to the church with bottles of turpentine to defend an inviting target from midnight paint artists. Typically, he extracted the last drop of publicity out of the incident by informing reporters that he was removing the board only under the strongest protest. He had got the message across. Newspapers all over the Federation had reproduced photographs of the board.

There was another message emanating from the town of Chingola besides that of blatant racial discrimination. In a press statement he declared:

'Sir Roy Welensky has frequently to apologize to visiting dignitaries from Asian and African States who fall foul of the Federation's colour bar. No doubt, when he feels moved to apologize for the treatment meted out not only to distingushed visitors but to our own humble African citizens, then he will have proved the sincerity of his partnership policy, but not until . . .'

Two years later, a police inspector whose daughter Morris had helped in a time of need rather shamefacedly confessed that he and a colleague had defaced the board. It had annoyed them so much as they drove past the church on night shift that they had tried to remove it, and when this failed, got a pot of paint and altered its message to one more in keeping with their feelings about the Chingola Free Church and its minister. Morris brushed the incident aside and they reminisced about the stirring days before the passing of the 1960 Race Relations Ordinance which finally outlawed the colour bar in public places. Morris's ceaseless agitation undoubtedly had its effect in pushing through the Bill. He never let the legislators forget for a moment the scandal and immorality of discriminatory practices. He gave the Bill a guarded welcome but warned: 'It is seven years too late. The African people are no longer interested in eating in European cafés. Their aims are now massively political. Once they have achieved self-rule, they will show less tender regard for the feeling of café and hotel proprietors than the drafters of this present legislation.'

'How can I convince you,' Morris once asked a hostile crowd of mine workers at a meeting in the Vega Cinema, Bancroft, 'that I am not a traitor to my race and my own people, that it is out of my agonizing concern for you and your future that I have tried to get you to face unpalatable facts? The patience of the African people is exhausted. Unless there is drastic change, and soon, we shall have here a racial holocaust that will make life not worth living for any of us. I predict that within the next five years there will be African government in Northern Rhodesia and how we behave now will determine our fate then.' His prediction was greeted with hoots of derision. Had not Sir Roy Welensky, the tough, ebullient hero of Central African Whites assured them that not in his lifetime would he allow any of the three Territories of the Federation to fall under the control of an African government? Four years after that speech, Kenneth Kaunda ruled an independent Zambia and Sir Roy was an unemployed politician.

Just as Morris failed to get Copperbelt Whites to accept his prediction about the speed of change in Africa, so he found it impossible to convince them that it was out of concern for them and their families, as much as his belief that the African people must have justice, that had led him to speak out. He was a White Kaffir, and that was all about it. Yet his record belies the charge that he was an uncritical admirer of everyone and everything Black. From the time when his name became legendary amongst Africans he used his influence and his powerful voice to draw attention to shortcomings also. He never saw the racial struggle as a kind of Morality Play in which the Whites were all devils and the Blacks angels. Black racialism was as abhorrent to him as the White variety. And even as he delivered his angry attacks on the colour bar, he also warned the victims of it to beware of using it as a warm cocoon in which to coddle their failures. Addressing a conference of African teachers in Ndola he commented: 'One of the more lunatic effects of the colour bar is that it enables some Africans to award themselves, metaphorically at least, the degree of B.A. (Never attempted). Many talented Africans hurl themselves against the colour bar to get recognition for their gifts. There are others, however, who find in racial discrimination a cast iron excuse for attempting nothing, achieving nothing, and arriving nowhere.'

Wherever Morris saw cruelty, injustice and oppression, he hit out at it regardless of its racial origin. And his straight

Colin Morris in action during his weekly 'Argument' programme on Zambia Television. *Photo: Mike Reed*

Three of Africa's most 'turbulent priests' – Michael Scott, Colin Morris and Merfyn Temple. *Photo: Maggie Senogles*

Alice Lenshina's cathedral at Sione, near Lubwa, where the final battle of the Lumpa uprising was fought. *Photo: Times of Zambia*

Alice Lenshina – 'I rose from the dead'. *Photo: Times of Zambia*

One of Alice's 'Passports to Heaven', which promises to turn Army bullets to water.

The result of a reprisal raid by Senga villagers on some of Lenshina's followers. Troops can be seen preparing a mass grave. *Photo: Central Press Photos Ltd.*

The other side of the coin. A handful of Zambian villagers lucky to escape with their lives after an attack by Lenshina's warriors. *Photo: Central Press Photos Ltd.*

talking made him enemies on the African side as well. A classical example was his attitude to the Monckton Commission, appointed by the British Government in 1960 to review the progress of the Federation. The nationalist movement decided to boycott the Commission and urged Africans not to give evidence before it. Morris thought this a mistake and said so with typical bluntness. He believed that, far from boycotting it, Africans should appear before it in their hundreds and let the distinguished Commissioners really feel the strength of their convictions about the injustice of the Federation. There was a sharp reaction from some African politicians. Mr Francis Chembe, an independent member of the Federal Parliament, attacked the Fighting Parson in the African press, using the precise argument White settlers had been hurling at Morris for years. Said Mr Chembe: 'Chingola's Fighting Parson should mind his own business, that of religion, and not involve himself in affairs that have to do with the African's future well-being. We are not going to be influenced by missionaries in our struggle for freedom. . .'

'Well,' commented Morris ruefully, reading a report of Chembe's attack, 'I just can't win! But I suppose if I've got both Blacks and Whites telling me to mind my own business, either I'm being magnificently objective or just plain contrary!' He was probably being a little of both. And it was his fierce independence of mind that resulted in his having to dodge fire from both sides as the battle-lines of the racial struggle were formed. He found himself as a result in the middle of one of the nastiest incidents in Northern Rhodesia's freedom struggle.

On 8th May, 1960, a mob of Africans, returning home after police had dispersed an unauthorized United National Independence Party meeting, attacked a White housewife, Mrs Lillian Burton, and her two children, who were passing along the road in her car. The car was stopped, doused with petrol and set alight. Mrs. Burton managed to push her two children out of the car, but she herself sustained burns from which she died. White settlers went wild. Mass meetings were held throughout the Copperbelt where Federal MPs and mineworkers' leaders demanded the banning of UNIP, the arming of White civilians and the deportation of certain individuals, notably Colin Morris, who were inciting Africans by their inflammatory speeches. As usual, the Fighting Parson was responsible for the very things he had predicted would happen. His daily crop of anonymous letters took an uglier turn from crazy abuse to outright charges that he had Mrs Burton's blood on his hands – 'I'll bet you're sorry her two children weren't burnt as well. If your murdering friends had got their way those two little White children would have been fried *black* THE WAY YOU LIKE THEM!'

Tension on the Copperbelt was at fever pitch. The two races retired to their townships, boiling with rage. Morris also had strong feelings about the murder of Mrs Burton, but he did not give vent to them from the safety of White mass meetings. He went into an African township and in a furious speech told an African crowd exactly how he felt. 'Those five minutes of insensate hate have closed doors that some of us have worked years to prise open. Is this the treatment that White women and children can expect if Europeans do the thing which some of us have been asking of them for years, relinquish their grip on political control? Are the proud African people reduced to this – taking out their hatred of the Government, the Federation, and the police on a woman?' Morris was heard in sullen silence by Africans seething under the wild threats being made by White extremists. He stalked out of the hall and drove home. The Man in the Middle – the loneliest place on earth.

Morris got no credit from the White community for his courage in addressing that meeting. Those who were aware that he had done it shrugged the whole thing off as his lame attempt to atone for the harm he had done by his irresponsible championing of the African cause. But the strength of feeling about the Burton murder did not deter him from protesting publicly a week later when the Governor of

Northern Rhodesia banned UNIP in the Western Province and restricted UNIP leaders Kaunda, Kapwepwe and Sipalo from visiting the Copperbelt. 'This is a fundamental mistake,' he argued. 'These are the only men who can control the African people. They are their chosen leaders. Cut them off from the nationalist movement on the Copperbelt and you will allow any thug or agitator free rein to fan the flames of racial hatred. This is not the way to prevent another Burton incident but to create the conditions that will lead to others!' 'There he goes again,' said White opinion with grim triumph, 'defending his Black friends when they murder an innocent White woman.' The trouble was that Morris was attempting to state a reasoned case to people who, in his own phrase, were now only capable of thinking with their blood.

He had a growing sense of alienation. He felt himself to be talking in a vacuum. He was no longer where the action was. The struggle was now totally political. The Church, he felt, had lost its chance to mediate. Politics, not preaching, was the way to get things done.

8

COLIN MORRIS's first foray into the arena of party politics had been brief and inconclusive, but it is worth recounting because it led to an act of desecration that shocked even the hardest-bitten Whites.

In October, 1957, a hundred people, Africans, Eurafricans, Asians and Europeans met at Lilanda Farm, home of Dr Alexander Scott, an independent member of the Federal Parliament, to inaugurate a new political party. Recognizing that the day of the Independent was drawing to a close, Scott was sounding out support for some kind of liberal political grouping that could bridge the growing gap between the two races and try to translate multi-racialism into political terms. Thus was born the Constitution Party, short-lived and appearing on the scene long before its time, yet a sign of things to come. The Party's chairman was the Rev. Merfyn Temple, fellow Methodist missionary and close friend of Colin Morris. After the meeting, he travelled to the Copperbelt to invite the Fighting Parson to join. Morris needed little persuasion, though he was not optimistic about the party's prospects. He recalls: 'I was heartily sick of being told by anxious missionaries and laymen that at all costs the Church must not be accused of taking sides in political issues. They did not seem to see that their neutrality was shoring up an oppressive *status quo*. Anyway, the Christian is surely the most partisan of men. He is vehemently *for* righteousness and *against* injustice wherever they are found. I was relieved to be able to stop moralizing about politics from the touch-line and get into the fray.'

Morris was only one of a number of parsons who joined the Constitution Party. Indeed, if the presence of clergy is a guarantee of respectability, it must have been the most reputable party in political history! Morris was not the only Political Parson but his joining inevitably caused the greatest stir. Wrote *Most Concerned* to the *Northern News:* 'It is shocking to read that the Rev. Morris has now started to use the House of God to serve his selfish political ambitions . . . . on top of everything else, this political egotist will now begin venting his nonsensical doctrines from the pulpit . . .'

Morris was well aware of the theoretical arguments against parsons getting involved in party politics and knew that he might divide the congregation at the point where he ought to unite them – the pulpit. He put the issue squarely before his Church Council. The result was a statement in the Church Newsletter signed by the Secretary which answered charges that the minister had been using his pulpit to recruit support for a political party:

'Mr Morris has the full support of his Church Council, who stand four square behind him in his gallant efforts to educate the thinking public of this Territory to an understanding of a Christian approach to our difficulties. He has never at any time used his pulpit for the expression of party political opinions. If what he says has political repercussions then this only serves to underline the power of his statement of the Christian case.

'Furthermore, in his endeavours to reconcile the races and point the Judgement of God upon those practices and customs of society which fall short of the Law of Christ, he is carrying out the policy of the Chingola Free Church, to which we all subscribe . . .'

Yet again, Colin Morris had cause to be thankful for the good sense and clear-sightedness of a remarkable group of Christians. Not that all their denials that he was using his pulpit for illicit political activity did much to abate the frenzied accusations levelled at him. But *he* felt much better for knowing that there were lay folk, some of whom almost certainly supported other political parties, who knew what he was driving at.

The Constitution Party did not long survive. It was a lone star that shot briefly across the heavens, a faint light-bearer soon gone. The bunch of individualists who made up its executive did little but argue amongst themselves, and in the first election the Party fought, it was crushingly defeated. But long before it got its *coup de grâce* through the ballot box, Morris was at odds with the majority of his fellow leaders. The Party had, at its first and only Convention, expressed guarded support for a radically reformed Federation. Morris and one or two others were absolutely convinced that the Party was doomed unless it declared its opposition to the Federation from the outset. He could not share the optimistic views of his colleagues that, given time, Federation could win widespread African support. It was a matter for political judgement. Morris happened to be right and before the Party folded up, more and more members, utterly defeated in their attempts to sell the idea of a reformed Federation to the African public, came to share his opinion.

Possibly the only real significance of the Constitution Party for Morris personally was that it led to an outspoken sermon on the rôle of the Church in politics, which in turn had the most horrifying repercussion.

Morris's attempts to sell the policy of a Party he only half-believed in were, for him, half-hearted, and much of his time in public meetings and house discussions was spent, not in arguing the liberal case, but in trying to convince disbelieving people that it was right for a minister of religion to express publicly any party political views at all. He decided to 'come clean' with his congregation in a widely advertised and reported sermon 'Politics – can the Church be Involved?' After dealing with the biblical evidence that supported positive political action, he declared that though it would be wrong to claim that God takes sides for or against any class or race He has a special concern for the outcast and the oppressed, expressed in Jesus' inversion

86

of the accepted standards of society so that those who are of negligible value in the world's eyes are exalted to a central position of regard. He went on:

'Translate this Gospel concern into political terms, and one conclusion is inescapable. Although we dare not claim that any political party is absolutely right and others are absolutely wrong, we can surely state on the authority of the Gospel that any political policy which is openly committed to perpetuating the domination of one race over another, and which denies the outcast his place in the sun, is defective and un-Christian. It is not enough to say it. We must take some action to placard the fact before the whole community. This certain parsons have done, by allying ourselves openly with the only party which is prepared to take positive action to fight for the rights of the under-privileged, and to translate this gospel concern into a political pressure. . . .

'Let me make this clear. I am trying to justify the Christian basis of my own political action. I am neither saying nor implying that any of you should join any particular political party. . . . .

'We "political parsons", as the press delights to call us, may be proved wrong, God help us. But our situation in Central Africa is so grave that it is better for the official representatives of the Church to be sincerely wrong through taking positive action than to be impeccably right though totally irrelevant by doing nothing . . .'[1]

The sermon, widely reported, produced the usual shoal of newspaper correspondence on the theme of the parson in politics. In summary, the views of most of the public boiled down to:

1. Parsons don't know anything about politics so should stick to the Bible.
2. 'Politics' means a discussion of any aspect of life in the real world as opposed to 'spiritual' subjects.

[1]Morris, *Out of Africa's Crucible*. Lutterworth, 1960, pp. 52–53.

3. Parsons ought not to lead but to follow the views of their people on such matters as Federation, etc.
4. He is preaching 'politics' if he challenges European racial views; he is preaching 'true' religion if he attacks African attitudes and behaviour.

Point 4 was amply proved by a report in the *Northern News* the week following Morris's sermon, that a Roman Catholic priest in Luanshya had delivered a slashing attack from the pulpit upon UNIP for its godlessness, and then, somewhat illogically, ordered his African congregation to make three days 'reparation'. The applause on the Copperbelt was deafening. Morris got at least a dozen letters enclosing the story-clipping with various bits of advice appended, mostly to the effect that here was a *real* minister. 'And the moral of this little story,' Morris commented, 'is that a parson ought not to take part in politics, but if he does, he'd better make certain he comes down on the Right Side!'

The debate on how far a parson dare go in involving himself in party politics rages in every corner of Christendom. But someone on the Copperbelt decided to take the debate a stage further. A few days after Morris had preached his sermon members of the congregation, arriving early for the Church's Annual General Meeting, found the church in an indescribable mess. During the hour between the departure of the African caretaker and their arrival someone had entered the church and smashed everything in sight. The communion table, inscribed, perhaps in this context ironically, 'Do this in Remembrance of Me', had been overturned and its beautiful carving chipped. The copper cross that always stood on it had been tossed into a pool of whitewash. Insults had been scrawled on walls and windows. Footprints on the communion rail indicated that someone had run along it. An aerosol tin of white spray, used for creating a winter effect on the Church's Christmas tree, had been used to write obscenities and indecipherable initials on any available wall or floor space.

Morris's vestry looked as though it had been bomb-blasted. Glass, chinaware, lamp bulbs and anything else easily breakable had been ground into his carpet. Hymn books and sheet music were shredded and scattered like some grotesque devil's confetti. His preaching robes had been drenched in communion wine, presumably the handiest substitute for blood.

Most significantly, the huge pulpit Bible, a gift from the local African churches, had been taken from the pulpit, dropped into the soggy mess, and the passage from which Morris had taken his sermon text for the Politics sermon had been cut and scored with a knife. His text was from the fifty-eighth chapter of Isaiah:

'Is not this the fast that I have chosen? to loose the bands of wickedness, to undo the heavy burdens, and to let the oppressed go free, and that ye break every yoke?'

All theories that the desecration was the work of children or irresponsible youths foundered on this one rock – that whoever the vandal was, he knew from which part of the Bible Morris had taken his text. And what might have been shrugged off as a terrible and senseless act of destruction had to be viewed in a more sinister light. Somewhere in the community was an enemy who would violate a church in his demented hatred of the Fighting Parson.

As the congregation filed in for the Annual General Meeting, they gazed on the gory mess, and then, abandoning the agenda, got to work with mops and sweeping brushes in an attempt to repair the ravages. Some of the damage was permanent. Ten years later, Colin Morris opens his tattered pulpit Bible every Sunday, its pages discoloured with communion wine, and, if he is reading from Isaiah, can gaze for an instant on the knife cuts – a permanent reminder that there can be a heavy price to be paid for an open Christian stand in an area of tension.

Morris, who had been ill in bed, was driven to the church the next morning to see the damage. As he walked through the main doors, he overheard a police inspector, dusting for fingerprints, say to a colleague, 'Serve the bastard right!' Did it really serve him right? he asked himself.

89

Had the greater act of desecration been his own in disregarding the traditional limits of the Church's involvement with the world? He experienced fully the aloneness of the controversialist, for how can he ever know that the harm he must inevitably do does not outweigh the good he sincerely believes will come from his actions? Though not a conventionally pious man, Morris, writing of the incident in *The Hour after Midnight*, tells how he recalled, as he surveyed the debris, an Elizabethan prayer, 'For Our Enemies', that he had once memorized as a neutralizer for his hot temper. He repeated it fervently, overawed and not a little frightened that he had the power to evoke such demented hate from someone that he or she was prepared to go to the lengths of desecration of a church to express it: 'Lord, we desire their amendment and our own . . . . separate them not from us by punishing them, but join and knot them to us by Thy favourable dealing with them . . .' Not easy words to say as he fingered his preaching gown stained with communion wine and the slashed Bible.

He had always feared that his crusade might bring harm upon his church in a spiritual sense, but never dreamt it would suffer such damage. Yet the senseless act had, in some indefinable way, sharpened the issue in his mind. The desecration was tangible proof that the Church was not engaged in some polite, academic discussion on the subject of Race, but in a crusade against Evil. He was engaged in no game, whose humour and drama were to be savoured, but in a mortal struggle that was laying bare the hatred and fear in the hearts of men. He stepped out of the church, feeling strangely at peace. The worst had now happened; the substance of his fears had proved less daunting than their shadow.

In the following days, he received numerous letters of sympathy. One came from the Chairman of the Nchanga branch of the African National Congress, offering to provide a round-the-clock guard for the Chingola Free Church, which he described as 'a holy place of love and tolerance in a land of hate and prejudice'. There was the odd anonymous letter, threatening to repeat the act, but on the whole his critics were, for a while, silenced. A few weeks later Morris met a well-known Copperbelt character who had taken the odd poke at him in the press, and commented that he had not seen any letters from him recently. 'What?' he replied indignantly, 'Have the whole Copperbelt thinking I was the one that smashed up your church?'

The police never discovered who had violated the Chingola Free Church. When a detective asked Morris whether he had any particular enemies, the Fighting Parson smiled grimly and handed him a copy of the Territory's telephone directory!

9

MORRIS did not regret his involvement with the Constitution Party. At the very least it taught him that there is a great difference between pronouncing upon political issues from the Olympian heights of the pulpit and having to wrestle with all the complexities and compromises involved with life in the actual political arena. It is possible to detect a less strident note in his public judgements upon the Federation's politicians from this time on. The clash of personalities, the balancing of conflicting interests, and the sheer hard slog of getting people of both races to act politically to the limit of what they professed all formed part of his apprenticeship to practical politics.

Meanwhile, he was glad to spend more time with the Chingola Free Church congregation which, he was astounded to note, was beginning to creep up to something like its former size. For one thing, the African families who attached themselves to the Church brought a cosmopolitan vigour to its life. For another, a serious stock-taking was going on in the minds of people who only a couple of years before would not have allowed themselves to come within range of Morris's voice. Amid all the confusion and rapidly changing circumstances the Fighting Parson had sounded a clear, consistent note which never wavered – 'change, change whilst there is still time, for what you are not prepared to offer willingly will be taken from you forcibly.' For the first time doubt began to creep into the minds of the more thoughtful Whites that *their* prophet, Sir Roy Welensky, would be able to hold back the Black tide. Events began to confound some of his predictions and confirm those of the Chingola parson. Maybe, too, there was a certain sporting admiration for a fighter who, no matter how hard you knocked him down, came up for more.

Noting this new awareness amongst a growing number of Europeans that Central Africa was moving towards some sort of crisis, Morris found that where he once was snubbed or howled down for the robust expression of his views, people began to single him out in order to vent upon him not their spite so much as their confusion. In some measure, this faint dawning of perception was some compensation for the heartaches of stormier days. As it was borne upon Whites that they could no longer regard the militant Black masses as some kind of optical illusion which, if they blinked their eyes, would go away, they began to wonder just what these Africans were really like, and they turned in the direction of one of the few people who could tell them. In the barber's shop, on the streets and on his house calls, Morris would find himself drawn with contrived artlessness into discussion on the one subject that before would have been avoided like the plague. 'What does the African want,' he would be asked, 'that we haven't already given him?' He could well have replied, 'Go and ask him!' but he would have scored only a cheap debating point for he knew perfectly well that not one European in a thousand would have the foggiest idea how to set about finding an African who could tell him. And such was the total break-down of communication between the races that few of those who *could* have answered such questions, *would* have done. For them the days of debate and polite discussion were long past. The time for action was approaching.

Of course, Europeans could have put these teasing questions to their trusted house servants who, over the colonial decades, have developed a genius for keeping *bwana* happy by producing the expected answers to loaded questions. The conversation would run something like this:

'You don't want a vote, do you Emmanuel?'

'Vote, *bwana*, what is that?' Emmanuel's face would crease into an innocent frown.

'You know . . . politics.'

'Oh no, *bwana*! Politics is no good for the African people.'

'What about these nationalists, then?'

'They bad men, *bwana* – cause much trouble.'

'So you're happy then, Emmanuel?'

'Oh, yes *bwana*. *Bwana* a good man, treat me well. I'm very happy.'

Emmanuel would smilingly resume his ironing whilst *bwana* went back to his iced lager, convinced that people like Colin Morris were irresponsible panic-merchants with all their talk of African patience being exhausted. *Bwana* might well have had a moment's unease if he had studied events in neighbouring Kenya where very often the first sight of Mau Mau White settlers got was of Emmanuel, their faithful retainer, charging into their dining room with a *panga* in his hands.

What did the African people want? In speeches and conversations and articles Morris patiently reiterated that they wanted many things – an end to human valuation on the grounds of colour, equality of economic opportunity, and political rights. But above all they were fighting for their self-respect and manhood. They wanted an end to a system built upon a single premise – that human dignity is something you were born with if you were White but which you must earn by your own efforts if you are Black. In one sermon he put it this way:

'Our whole philosophy of life here is based upon a dual system of values. There are 'good' Europeans and 'bad' Europeans, 'good' Africans and 'bad' Africans. The words 'good' and 'bad' have no common reference as between the two races. When the European housewife or shift-boss refers to an African as a 'good boy', this is shorthand for 'he's pretty good *for an African*'. It is the noun that classifies him and determines his fate; the adjectives 'good', 'bad' or 'indifferent' merely indicate the degree of approval he is entitled to get from Europeans. Because Europeans treat good Africans better than bad Africans, they contrive by some form of mental acrobatics to convince themselves that they are judging their Black fellow citizens solely on their merits as *men*. They are not; they are judging them as *Africans*. The social structure of our society is built upon the nouns – African, European, Asian – rather than upon the adjectives – good, bad, or indifferent – therefore it is a static society. For you can change the adjectives by education, culture, or religion: the nouns are immutable – categories of absolute classification.'

Jomo got the point; many didn't. Morris and those like him who could see that this static society was about to be swept by the hurricane power of nationalism talked and argued and pleaded, uneasily conscious that events were rapidly overtaking their words. And it was the blindness of the politicians that baffled him. He could understand the average White settler being unable to see that current policies were bound to lead to a violent racial collision, but the politicians were without excuse. The Federal and Territorial Governments went merrily on their way to doom, not merely oblivious to the ominous signs rising like smoke signals from the African townships but adding provocation to complacency by hedging in nationalist leaders such as Kenneth Kaunda within webs of legal restriction – they were harried and spied on and imprisoned on any pretext; they were prevented from moving freely around their own land; their homes were raided, their speeches recorded. A defiant procession of nationalists trooped in and out of the Federation's prisons. Men like Andrew Mutemba and Fines Bulawayo, both friends of Morris, went to gaol no less than eleven times. 'This is madness!' Morris would explode, 'You are not giving the policy of non-violence a chance. How long do you expect the African people to remain quiet and accept the constant humiliation of their leaders without retaliation?' His debating opponent would snort and evoke a rousing cheer from the White audience as he declared, 'Non-violence! Do you expect us to believe the word of thugs who burned a European woman alive?' Not well received was Morris's rejoinder that Whites had no option but to trust these pacifist nationalist leaders unless they preferred to deal with some of their lieutenants who were making no secret of their desire to call the African people to a Holy War.

Privately, Morris was expressing in letters to British M.P.s and his Missionary Society headquarters doubts about the practicability of Kenneth's Kaunda's non-violent, passive resistance policy – not because he had the slightest misgiving about Kaunda's sincerity, but because he felt that too many factors were outside the control of the Nyasaland parson's son who had become the acknowledged leader of the nation's freedom struggle. 'Kenneth's fighting history, not Welensky,' he wrote. 'Africans know perfectly well that it's only when the violence starts that a colonial power takes their demands seriously . . . Egypt, Malaya, Cyprus, Indonesia, the Congo – the story is always the same – reasonable words about non-violence are always shrugged off: violence itself never is. All the time the Government's breathing fierce threats about the dire consequences of violence, it is, by its refusal to negotiate, driving the nationalist leaders to the point where they have no alternative to violence.'

He told an audience in Ndola's Lowenthal Theatre: 'No African leader has the slightest chance of withstanding violent pressures from his rank and file unless he can show tangible evidence that non-violence *works*. To this simple fact, our Government has chosen to blind itself. By refusing to acknowledge the official existence of these leaders, let alone sit round a table with them, it is merely proving the point being made by militant elements in the nationalist movement that non-violence does not pay . . .'

Then he uttered the ultimate heresy that earned him a resounding thunder of 'Boos':

'As you sit in this theatre, your safety and security are not vested in the hands of the police or the Federal Army. You are under the protection of Kenneth Kaunda. As long as he leads the African people, you are safe. But should he be overthrown, or quit in disillusionment, all the guns in the Federation could not protect you. Do you want to live in a society where you must carry revolvers at your hip, have bars over your bedroom windows; in which your children cannot walk down the street in safety; where a dark cloud of fear hangs over everything; where you jump at every sound? That is the shape of your future unless the Government comes to terms with Kaunda and his demands. If Kaunda falls, you will be a beleaguered little White island surrounded by a great pounding sea of Black nationalism. And Kaunda *must* fall unless he can show his people that non-violence pays.'

It was both up-hill and utterly depressing to be Northern Rhodesia's Prophet of Doom. Sir Roy Welensky referred to Morris in a public speech as a 'Dismal Jeremiah'. Morris's retort was swift, and biting: 'Sir Roy doesn't know his Bible very well. Jeremiah was proved right, and those who didn't listen to him perished.'

'Take a holiday,' suggested Morris's Church Council, a prospect likely to fill him with greater gloom than a prison sentence since he had, and has, no hobbies, no relaxing pastimes to take his mind off the demands of his job. But it was sound advice. He was getting stale and the toll of his life of controversy was beginning to show. He was nervy, easily depressed, even more restless than normal, and unable to sleep.

He went off to Britain for a month, grimly determined to read nothing but paper-back thrillers and to keep his mind firmly off Africa and its problems. And he might have succeeded, had he not met up with one of Britain's most remarkable women, Mrs Barbara Castle, that year Chairman-Designate of the Labour Party and a staunch supporter of the African cause. He was unable to resist an invitation to address a meeting in Blackburn, her constituency. The fiery red-head and the Fighting Parson would be a formidable combination on any platform. That night they did a real hatchet-job on the Federation; and

97

one phrase of Morris's, which was the main headline in most Central African newspapers next morning, afterwards became part of Africa's political vocabulary, endlessly quoted, generally without acknowledgement of its source. Referring to the Federation's official racial policy, he roundly declared, 'Partnership is the biggest confidence trick in modern political history.' Morris was in trouble again. In Salisbury, Southern Rhodesia, the Federal Minister of Law, Mr Julian Greenfield, took the occasion of a Rhodes Day ceremony to accuse Morris of a 'wicked attack' and added that 'the Federal Government has no intention of allowing the calumnies of people like him to deflect us from our task of building up a harmonious nation out of our diverse elements. Nothing will stop our advance to free independent nationhood.' Morris was unimpressed. Shown Greenfield's statement by reporters in London he said flatly that the Federal Government's policies were sub-Christian, that he couldn't support them, and that any Christian who did ought either to examine his conscience or get someone suitably qualified to examine his head.

Morris came back to face the storm. On his way through Salisbury, Federal Immigration and Customs Officers at the airport gave him a thorough working-over to demonstrate their disapproval, searching and subjecting him to sufficient inconvenience to ensure that he missed his plane to Ndola. 'To this day,' confesses Morris, 'I get a tight feeling whenever I have to go through customs and immigration at Ndola Airport.' These days he is likely to be ushered straight through by smiling Zambians, but the psychological blockage still remains, a legacy of the time when a customs examination was more likely to be an ordeal of petty persecution than a formality.

'The next time you go on holiday,' said the late Jonathan Barnes, his Church Treasurer, 'we'll send someone with you – with a gag!'

Though he was again, as usual, a storm centre of controversy, Morris's mental attitude was different. He had a buoyancy and self-confidence that some of his friends once feared had been hammered out of him. He no longer had a despairing sense of 'bashing away at a great rock with a feather duster,' as he once put it. In London he had detected signs that the British Government could not ignore African demands much longer. The anti-Federation lobby inside Parliament and outside it was growing. And one needed no microscope to detect the cracks in the edifice of Federation that resulted from the smashing blows of the nationalist leaders who, unlike him, had something more substantial than a feather duster at their disposal – the united will of millions of Nyasaland and Northern Rhodesian Africans.

Whites still seemed firmly in control of political power, but the trend of Morris's speaking and writing was towards shaping the day after tomorrow when Federation would be a bad dream and Africans would have the responsibilities as well as the right to rule their own country. He told a congregation in a Bancroft African church that 'although the European is at present your guardian, in the very near future you will be the guardian of the European.' This prediction earned him a stern rebuke from the *Northern News*. Wrote its Editor:

'Colin Morris is a sincere campaigner on behalf of the under-privileged. He has taken the cause of Africans to heart and is determined to help them in every way open to him. But we believe he is going about it the wrong way. In his sermon to an African congregation he mixed sound common sense with some of the most misleading advice which his audience can ever expect to hear. . . . When he speaks of Africans becoming the guardians of the Europeans in the near future, he is being irresponsible and mischievous.

'What can be the effect of such words upon an African congregation, many of them simple folk, who have no pretensions to power and glory? Do they imagine themselves suddenly being transformed into the leaders, or perhaps sole owners of this country, and soon, too, for that is how they will interpret 'near future'. That may be what the Rev. Morris would like to see, but it does not reflect the Constitution of the Federation or the meaning of Partnership. It is something of his own imagination.' Imagination?

Federation was dead and buried just two years later.

In 1957, Frank Barton, at that time Editor of the *African Times*, the only pro-nationalist newspaper of its day, had taken Colin Morris along to Chilenji Township to meet the man who, in his opinion, would one day lead the African people of Northern Rhodesia. At that time Kenneth Kaunda was Secretary-General of the African National Congress, whose President was Harry Nkumbula. This was the year that Kaunda and Nkumbula went to London to plead the cause of self-rule, and got little but a polite hearing. Re-called Kaunda, 'We seemed to be getting nowhere at all. Harry Nkumbula lost his sense of direction, and I thought of giving up politics altogether.'[1]

The split between the two men grew. Younger, brighter, and more militant nationalists began to look towards the austere Kaunda for the leadership the easy-going, good-living Nkumbula had ceased to provide. The breaking point came when Nkumbula agreed to support a Constitution for Northern Rhodesia, named after the Colonial Secretary, Lennox Boyd, which Kaunda and his supporters, notably .Simon Kapwepwe, now Vice-President of the Republic of Zambia, thought was totally unsatisfactory in the representation it gave the African people. The rebels walked out of the National Council of the African National Congress and in October, 1958, formed the Zambia African National Congress with Kaunda as President. It was the beginning of political eclipse for Nkumbula and a meteoric journey for Kaunda from a mud house on a Lubwa mission station to State House, Lusaka.

Neither the nationalist leader nor the Fighting Parson recall that 1957 meeting as being one where each made anything more than a favourable impression upon the other.

[1]Hall, *Kaunda, Founder of Zambia*, Longmans Green, 1964.

But as the years of the freedom struggle wore on, they were to become firm friends. When, in 1959, Sir Arthur Benson, the Governor of Northern Rhodesia, banned the Zambia African Congress and restricted Kaunda and his close associates to a bleak detention camp in Kabompo, Morris wrote to him and initiated a correspondence which became a debate continuing to the present day on political problems – a debate whose ultimate fruit was a book: *A Humanist in Africa*, published by Longmans Green in 1966, in which the philosophy of the nationalist leader, now Head of State, was set out in a series of letters carefully edited by Morris. But in 1959 their correspondence was concerned with more mundane things: 'I am very concerned about the problem of excessive drinking amongst the African people,' began Kaunda's first letter to Morris from Kabompo. It was the moralist as much as the politician in Kaunda who appealed to Morris.

And in 1960 there issued from their joint authorship a book afterwards described as a 'landmark in the freedom struggle' – *Black Government*. The original idea was Merfyn Temple's, who, besides being a political parson, was also Field Secretary for the United Society of Christian Literature, and who felt there was need for the views of these two remarkable men to be subjected to the judgement and analysis of the other. Kenneth Kaunda arrived at Morris's manse, looking haggard and ill, still unrecovered from a debilitating illness that almost killed him at Kabompo. He was accompanied by Fines Bulawayo, a local official of the Party, who kept watch outside the manse for the police, and Frank Chitambala, Kaunda's private secretary, who sat stolidly in the lounge guarding the contents of his leader's brief case and keeping a wary eye on Morris's Alsatian, Liz, who was keeping more than a wary eye on him. The manuscript, dictated in an afternoon to Morris's secretary, was taken off to Lusaka by Temple, and after a meal, Kaunda moved on to the next stage of his seemingly endless war of wits against the Government and police. *Black Government*, printed locally in Ndola against the hazards of printers threatening to strike rather than set the type and snooping Special Branch men reading the proofs before Temple got his hands on them, was an immediate best-seller – among Africans. Europeans thought the book seditious and plain silly, especially the paragraphs written by Morris, and headlined by the *Northern News*, in which he expressed his conviction that Kenneth Kaunda would be Prime Minister of an independent Northern Rhodesia within five years.

Black Government was to have two consequences, apart from the impact it made upon the thinking of Africans and a few reflective Europeans. It nailed together the names of Kaunda and Morris in the public mind in more than authorship – to the point where Morris was to be held responsible for the words and deeds of his nationalist friend in the eyes of Europeans. Not that Morris was anything other than proud of the association: 'I am proud to call Kenneth Kaunda a friend,' he wrote in a letter to the *Northern News* – a statement greeted with incredulity by Whites for whom all nationalist leaders were by definition thugs and terrorists. But it had its uncomfortable moments, as for example when Kaunda, utterly in despair at the double-dealing of the British Government at the 1961 Constitutional Conference, warned that they were creating a situation which would lead to an African reaction 'compared with which Mau Mau would seem like a Sunday School picnic'. Welensky chose to regard Kaunda's statement as a threat rather than a warning, and without consultation with Northern Rhodesia's Governor, moved Federal troops into Northern Rhodesia. Morris's share of the fall-out was a degree of abuse that could not have been greater had he made the statement himself.

The other consequence of *Black Government* was that Morris became a 'security risk'. Where before the police had kept a listless eye on him, largely because it seemed likely that angry Whites would sooner or later lynch him, now his open link with Kaunda was seen to mark a more sinister turn in his career – his house was kept under police surveillance, his mail was opened and, from time to time, his telephone was tapped. It became a pastime amongst journalists to lay bets on how long Morris would last before being deported. Under a headline 'How Long Can He Last?' Frank Barton, in an editorial in the *African Times*, commented:

'What a wonderful stand the Fighting Parson is taking against colour prejudice and repression. But can he last? Either in the Church or the country? As the pace quickens in the struggle for power, it may prove too big an embarrassment to have him around. One thing is certain. Until the day he is removed from either the country or the Church, Colin Morris, with the Bible in one hand and waving the other, clenched, in the face of hypocrisy, will go on fighting for the eight million underdogs of the Federation.'

From the vantage-point of 1968, when His Excellency, Dr K. D. Kaunda, President of the Republic of Zambia, and the Rev. Colin Morris, President of the United Church of Zambia, shrug off their burdens and retire to the verandah of State House to play table tennis, old allies as rivals in an unusual conflict between Church and State, the hard days must seem like a bad dream.

But in 1960 there was still a long road to travel.

10

1960 WAS A remarkable year in the history of Northern
Rhodesia. After a quiet opening, everything suddenly began
to happen at once. Change symbolized for years by the
trickling of a few stones suddenly burst forth in a fully-
fledged avalanche. The Race Relations Ordinance, outlawing the colour bar in public places, was put on the statute
book, and there were ugly scenes on the Copperbelt as
Africans first exercised their right to enter cafés, cinemas
and hotels. They were set upon by gangs of White youths,
and the police found themselves in the novel situation of
having to defend the rights of Black citizens against the
assaults of White ones. On the industrial front there were
also advances as proposals hammered out over long months
by the Joint Industrial Council for the Mining Industry
were accepted by the European Mineworkers' Union, and
the way opened for African workers to take a modest step
forward beyond the pick-and-shovel levels of the industry.

Federation was rocked by the proposal in the report of
the Monckton Commission that any of the three Territories
wishing to do so should be allowed to secede, and the British
Colonial Office was spelling out a new pattern of development for their East and Central African dependencies that
boded ill for the future of White political supremacy . . .
first Kenya, then Nyasaland were granted Constitutions
providing for African majorities in their Legislatures, in
spite of the frenzied protests of their White communities.
And Mr Macleod, the Colonial Secretary, having closed the
file on Nyasaland, began to cast his eye over Northern
Rhodesia. There could be little doubt what he saw – the
need for an end to constitutional wrangling and interim

solutions that always failed; the Territory must be set forward on its way once and for all towards Black rule.

Politically, the scene was set for a transitional period as power passed from Whites to Blacks; a difficult and dangerous time when it seemed that only some degree of racial harmony could forestall a violent conflagration. But a great gulf yawned between the two races. The United Federal Party, which enjoyed the support of the majority of Whites, remained to the bitter end loyal to its Federal leader, Sir Roy Welensky, and utterly resistant to any idea of Black rule 'for the foreseeable future'. On the other side of the chasm, Kenneth Kaunda's United National Independence Party, which had the universal support of all Africans except those in the southern areas of Northern Rhodesia who retained their trust in Nkumbula's African National Congress, was becoming increasingly restive under a fair degree of police provocation and Federal interference in the Territory's affairs.

It looked as though the brief day of the liberal-minded of both races had dawned as a transitional political force to superintend the peaceful transfer of power from one race to the other. Unfortunately, just at the time when this opportunity presented itself, the Central African Party, the only live liberal force in the Federation, disintegrated after its leader, Mr Garfield Todd, former Southern Rhodesia Premier, signed a letter addressed to the British Government appealing for the suspension of the Southern Rhodesia Constitution and armed intervention by British forces. Whether Todd was right or wrong, and in the light of the present impasse over UDI, the British Government might now have cause to regret the fact that their predecessors did not take his advice. The reaction of Europeans in the two Rhodesias was so violent that the Central Africa Party was shattered by it. In any case, the Northern wing of the Party, led by Sir John Moffat and boasting three Members in the Legislature, was finding the link with Southern Rhodesia to be an embarrassment in its efforts to win African support.

The way seemed open for a new initiative in the North and groups of liberals in the Territory met to discuss possible bases for action. On two things they were agreed. Any new party needed the stature and wisdom of Sir John Moffat, but also dynamic leadership expressed in a personality who had the 'crowd-magic' that Sir John, with all his virtue, lacked. It was generally agreed that Colin Morris was the only man who could provide it. If Sir John was acknowledged leader of the liberals who had formed the Central Africa Party, Morris was the equally acknowledged leader of those liberals who had remained outside it. Mutual friends arranged a meeting between Moffat and Morris, who found little difficulty in agreeing upon what was the necessary basis for liberal action – a party which would work itself out of a job in favour of the nationalists as soon as possible, and at the same time fight for the security of the Whites as a minority group in an independent Northern Rhodesia.

Morris had his problems. Temperamentally he was all for following his friend Merfyn Temple by throwing in his lot with Kaunda's UNIP – all that held him back was the hope that it might be possible to act within the White community to move Europeans sufficiently far 'left' to make the gap narrower between the two races. And he knew that open commitment to UNIP would put him so 'far out' as to be impotent in the rôle of any kind of mediator. He enjoyed the most cordial relationship with Kenneth Kaunda and the other nationalist leaders who respected his desire to attempt to bridge the gap rather than jump right over to the Black side of the chasm.

There was also the Chingola Free Church to consider. Morris did not feel he could face the crisis of yet another 'political priest' episode which would inevitably again shatter the hard-won unity of the fellowship sorely tried by the tremendous upheavals caused by his stand on racial discrimination, his assoication with the Constitution Party, and other controversial matters. This time he knew that he could not hold political activity and pastoral work in balance. It had to be one or the other – the pulpit or the platform. He put the problem to his battle-tried friends on the Church Council. To his surprise, they were virtually unanimous in their opinion that he should be where the action was, which they agreed was the political arena for the momentous months ahead. They also recognized that he would be fighting with one hand tied behind his back if he tried to win political support and at the same time weather the inevitable storm that yet another Morris foray into politics must provoke while he remained a parish minister.

The biggest question mark concerned his ministerial status. As a missionary, his boss was the Methodist Church in Great Britain, which had given generous and ungrudging support to his previous activities, even on one occasion brusquely rejecting requests from ecclesiastical leaders on the spot in Northern Rhodesia that he be removed for 'disturbing the peace of the Church and causing dissention amongst its people' – a request hotly followed up by a threat from African members of the Church that if Morris *were* removed, they would walk out. Whilst the British Methodist Church, with its strong tradition of social action, had supported his political activity as a necessary out-working of his pastoral ministry, the question was: what would their attitude be if he wished to become a full-time politician and still remain on the roll of ministers?

Morris put his request for 'Permission to Serve' (as the quaint phrase is) as a full-time politician to the President of the Methodist Conference. He was fortunate. The President that particular year, the Rev. Edward Rogers, was one of the Church's experts on political and social matters, with a keen grasp of affairs in the Federation. Mr Rogers also received for consideration at the same time as Morris's request a resolution from the Northern Rhodesia Synod of the Methodist Church that Morris should not be allowed to enter full-time politics. Mr Rogers, whilst recognizing the fears that underlay the Synod resolution, felt the situation in Central Africa to be so critical that Morris should be given freedom to act as he thought best. So Morris became one of the few Methodist ministers, if not the only one, ever allowed to serve as a full-time politician without forfeiting his ministerial status.

Fortified by the blessing and permission of the President of the Methodist Conference, the Fighting Parson regretfully took leave of his congregation. A Canadian missionary, the Rev. Charles Catto, was appointed Minister of the Chingola Free Church. Because church housing accommodation in Chingola was more than adequate Morris was allowed to stay on in his old manse on a rent-paying basis. So whatever chances and changes might befall him in the coming months he would at least still be surrounded by his old friends and also, he hoped, have the opportunity of sitting amongst his old congregation on the odd Sunday, even though he would no longer be the occupant of the pulpit.

As he sadly gathered together his belongings from the vestry that was no longer his, indulging in one of his genuine, if a tiny bit dramatized, fits of despair, Arthur Short assured him, 'Don't worry. You'll be back!' And eighteen months later, so he was. But what an eighteen months!

People of all races gathered in Kitwe for the inaugural meeting of the Liberal Party. Sir John Moffat was elected President; Morris, Deputy Leader and Senior Vice-President; Harry Franklin, a veteran liberal, Chairman; and Alfred Gondwe, Junior Vice-President. It was a brave occasion as liberals dedicated themselves at a time of great tension to express a political philosophy based upon a rejection of racial categories. Many of Morris's friends, veterans of a thousand battles, were represented in the local offices of the Party. Nobody under-estimated the Herculean task that faced them in attempting to win support across the racial divide, but there was sober optimism that if any combination could do it, Moffat and Morris were the men.

Sir John Moffat, great-grandson of the pioneer missionary, had spent all his life in Northern Rhodesia and had a distinguished record of public and government service. Knighted in 1955 for his work in pioneering the Moffat Resolutions on closer racial co-operation through the Northern Rhodesia legislature, he had later gone to the Federal Assembly in Salisbury as Chairman of the African Affairs Board. Returning to the Territorial Legislature as Member for the Eastern Rural constituency in 1959, he had been a principal architect of the 1960 legislation banning the colour bar.

In his study of the independence struggle, *Zambia, the Politics of Independence 1957–1964*,[1] David C. Mulford describes Moffat as 'somewhat doctrinaire, lacking both colour and the common touch'. This is a harsh judgement. Certainly Moffat found the cut and thrust of politics distasteful and his unduly quiet voice and carefully articulated speeches, which were symphonies of logic but hardly robust stuff, were not crowd-pleasers. The strength of the alliance between the Olympian Moffat and the ebullient Morris was seen to be a balancing of Moffat's sagacity and long experience with Morris's colour and fire. And from the beginning, though Morris and Moffat were never close, they had a mutual appreciation of each other's strengths and weaknesses. Moffat planned the strategy and delighted in constitutional discussion with Governors and Colonial Secretaries. Morris organized the Party, provided the oratory and put across policy in colourful, down-to-earth language. He saw to it that the Liberal Party was rarely out of the headlines. It was an arrangement that worked admirably for so long as Morris felt that Moffat's strategy was sound.

Between Morris and Moffat's old associate Harry Franklin, there was little love lost. Neither was responsible for an unhappy state of affairs. It was one of those clashes of temperament that frequently occurs in politics, though the Liberal Party was too small to be able to afford personal tension between two of its leaders. There were those, especially among Morris's friends, who felt that Sir John held

[1]Oxford University Press, 1967.

aloof and allowed his two colleagues to fight out their differences, loyalty to his old comrade inhibiting him from giving the new second-in-command his due place. And it must be confessed, Morris was a difficult man either to keep up with or work alongside – a natural leader accustomed for years to a free-ranging lone wolf rôle, he did not make an easy Deputy-Anything.

But personal tensions were an irrelevance compared with the glittering opportunity apparently presented to the new Party by the Lancaster House Constitutional Conference, called by Macleod for January 1961. The Liberal Party Executive worked out proposals, probably more ingenious than realistic, that would allow them to take advantage of their cross-sectional support. These proposals were based upon the introduction of voting qualifications designed to reflect the balance between the two races in the urban areas, with a system of reserved seats for the rural areas in which, for each constituency, an African and a European would be returned, each of whom must attract a given percentage of support from the opposite race. Ideally, this would produce a Legislature with a large African majority and the Liberal Party winning enough of the multi-racial seats to hold a balance of power.

Moffat, Morris, Franklin and Gondwe went off to London to put their views to the British Government. They found themselves playing a starring role at the Lancaster House Conference because the United Federal Party, on orders from Sir Roy Welensky, boycotted it. Liberals were thus the only non-nationalists present and the only group with any mandate on behalf of the White community, albeit a slender one. After the usual constitutional wrangling, Macleod offered a scheme which appeared to favour the Liberals as the transitional group. His proposal, which in its complexity somewhat reflected his bridge-playing genius, was for a three-decker Legislature comprising fifteen Lower Roll seats the Africans were certain to win, fifteen Upper Roll seats which the UFP would take, and fifteen National seats, ostensibly a gift to the Liberals, in which each candidate to be successful had to poll a minimum percentage of votes from both races.

The Liberal delegation returned from London delighted with the outcome of the Conference. Their jubilation was short-lived. Sir Roy Welensky, aided by a powerful pro-Federation lobby in the House of Commons, created such a furore that the scheme was drastically modified. When the Constitution was finally announced in February, 1962, by the new Colonial Secretary, Reginald Maudling, the Liberals found to their dismay that though the three-tier skeleton had been retained, the qualifications for the National seats had been raised to the extent that it looked impossible for anyone to meet them, Liberal or otherwise.

Putting their discouragement to one side, the Party went into action to win support for the forthcoming elections. Morris was in his element. Rowdy public meetings were meat and drink to him, and the mention of his name on the bill was enough to ensure a full house. Round the Copperbelt and the line of rail as far as Lusaka the Party circus went, Sir John delivering his carefully worded theses, packed with hard sense for those who took the trouble to listen closely. Morris provided the oratory, the stirring appeals, and the humour. He dealt with hecklers in devastating fashion, capping their quips to such effect that the crowd roared at their discomfiture. He was still the pressman's dream, pouring out highly quotable phrases. Night after night, in school halls and cinemas, he delighted the crowds with his virtuoso performances. It's doubtful if one in every hundred had the slightest intention of voting for the Liberal Party when the crunch came. They just loved to hear him talk!

Party supporters dug deeply into their pockets to pay for a clever newspaper advertising campaign that Morris master-minded. Since the official policy of the *Northern News* was to support the UFP, Morris paid for space and flooded it with cartoons, quips and, occasionally, a serious statement of Liberal Party policy. There was little doubt that the campaign was having its effect. The minutes of a

UFP Executive Meeting held in Broken Hill, wrongly addressed, fell into the hands of a Liberal Party member who brought them to Morris. They contained a series of comments expressing grave concern at the effect the Liberal Party's public meetings and newspaper advertisements were having upon UFP morale, and the Chairman complained that the Liberals must be employing a better public relations firm than the UFP were. Morris was the entire Liberal Party public relations set-up, capitalizing his years of experience in dealing with the press and his understanding of European psychology.

Publicly, the Liberal Party was going great guns. Privately, there was a growing division of opinion between Moffat and Morris about the Party's attitude to Kaunda's UNIP. Morris was convinced that a Liberal–UNIP alliance was essential if the seats requiring support from both races should not be void. He also felt that it would be a fatal error for the Liberals to fight UNIP for the Lower Roll Seats, not only because of the nationalist party's overwhelming African support but also because it would taint the Liberal Party as being anti-African nationalist in orientation. Morris's plan was that the Liberals should support UNIP for the Lower Roll seats, fight the UFP on the Upper Roll seats and operate in alliance with UNIP for the National seats. Moffat and Franklin, on the other hand, were convinced that they could recruit sufficient centre support to win the National seats and acquit themselves well on the Lower Roll. But then much of Moffat's and Franklin's time was spent in the Legislature. Morris, on the other hand, travelling around the country, organizing and speaking at the grass roots level, had a surer finger on the popular pulse, and was convinced that any anti-UNIP Liberal electoral action would ensure the eclipse of the Party. He proved to be one hundred per cent right.

The sequel to this sharp division within the Party on basic strategy is best told in the words of an academic student of Zambian politics, David Mulford:

'The Liberal Party was not free from internal strife.

On two occasions the disagreement became public and involved a conflict between Moffat and Morris. The more serious of these was in early 1962 over the question of co-operation with African nationalist parties. Moffat, who wished to avoid becoming involved in rivalry between UNIP and the African National Congress refused to consider co-operating with either party unless they united, a completely impracticable suggestion at best. On the other hand, Moffat's Vice-President, Rev. Colin Morris, favoured an immediate alliance with UNIP, arguing that the new Constitution made it essential that UNIP be not isolated from the European community during the coming election. Morris accordingly began private discussions with Kaunda, first to explore the possibility of an election alliance, and failing that, to propose an arrangement between a private group of Europeans and UNIP. On 12th March the conflict between Moffat and Morris became public. Despite the fact that Moffat himself had known about Morris's talks with Kaunda, the Liberal executive publicly dissociated itself from Morris's activities and he subsequently resigned, followed shortly afterwards by the Party's able young secretary, Denis Acheson. . . .'[1]

It was at this point that the personality clashes of the past took their toll in the Liberal Party. Moffat was inclined to ignore, though not support, Morris's approach to Kaunda, but his closest associates felt that the matter should be brought to a head and Morris disciplined. The party executive was split down the middle on the issue, regarding both Moffat and Morris, in their very diverse ways, as essential to the Party's fortunes. The policy difference represented between Moffat and Morris was one of those dilemmas which were the raw stuff of Liberal politics in Africa. Befogged though the matter was with personal clashes, Morris was quite clear that any Liberal Party that fought UNIP at the Election would have to do so without him. His supporters urged him to make a bid for the leadership of the

[1] D. Mulford, *Zambia, The Politics of Independence 1957–64*, Clarendon Press.

Party. Morris, though convinced that Moffat was wrong in his attitude to UNIP, and further, was greatly over-estimating his personal following amongst Africans, had great respect for him and baulked at a contest for power. Election time was fast approaching, and whether Morris won or lost a play-off against Moffat, and the chances were that it would be a stale-mate with the Party divided down the middle, the damage to the Party would be irreparable. Moffat had so often in the past proved right that Morris felt it would be unforgivable of him to wreck the Party when it was on the verge, in Moffat's view, of a resounding victory at the polls. He resigned, first his office, and then his membership of the Party. He was a lone wolf again. A number of his supporters resigned with him, and it was a greatly weakened Liberal Party that faced the election. Though some who remained were relieved to be rid of him, without Morris the Party lacked colour and flair. Its doleful end is soon told. All Liberal candidates were defeated, 28 out of 30 losing their deposits, and the Party secured less than 5 per cent of the total vote. Amongst those who lost their deposits were both Moffat and Franklin, and Sir John, bitterly hurt – and with some reason – at the poor support from Africans after a life-time of service on their behalf, announced his intention of returning to his Mkushi farm 'to watch the sun set from my verandah.'

The overall voting produced a deadlocked position between Kaunda's UNIP and the UFP with a number of ANC members holding the balance of power. Nkumbula, the ANC leader, decided to throw in his lot with his old enemy, and Northern Rhodesia moved into a phase of coalition government under African control. The day Morris had long predicted had at last arrived.

Morris decided to see the election through as an Independent. With typical generosity, Kaunda offered him a constituency on the National Roll and as the results of the voting indicated, had he accepted he would have won a Parliamentary seat. But after talking the matter over with his close friends, he decided to fight as an Independent on his home ground in Chingola. UNIP decided against putting a candidate up against him, and advised their supporters to back him. To choose Chingola, of every constituency in the country, was a calculated risk. On the one hand he had a hardy band of supporters who would work themselves into the ground for him. On the other, Chingola was the home of all his old enemies, every one of whom would count it a privilege to go along to the polling station for the pleasure of claiming a share in his defeat. In strict political terms, Morris's refusal of Kaunda's offer was certainly an error. If his aim was to get into Parliament, this was the only way he could do it. But there was still that dogged, some would say mulish, determination to give Whites one last chance of facing up willingly to the shape of their future. If he could pull it off, it would symbolize something immensely important; that some Whites, at least, were prepared to trust their future to Kaunda.

The UFP put up a Copperbelt lawyer, Mr Val Magnus, against Morris. The story of the election can be expressed in one sentence – Morris drew the crowds, Magnus got the votes. Although the UFP was confident of winning all 15 of the Upper Roll seats, it did let it be known that it was more than worried about Chingola. A procession of Party dignatories descended upon the town to address meetings. With the exception of Sir Roy Welensky, they drew poor audiences. If you were interested at all in election meetings, then those of the Fighting Parson were where the exitement was.

Morris fought the election on a simple two point statement:

1. Federation is finished. Get Northern Rhodesia out of it as soon as possible before the damage to her economy becomes crippling.

and . . .

2. An African majority in Northern Rhodesia's Legislature is inevitable. Better elect Whites to it who can

establish good relations with the Nationalists rather than the UFP who have a long record of animosity towards them.

The UFP platform was in many ways the direct contrary of Morris's position. It stood for support for Sir Roy Welensky in his efforts to keep the Federation intact, and for last ditch opposition to an African majority in the Territorial Legislature. But an ugly note was introduced into the campaign by a series of alarmist pamphlets calculated to play upon the worst fears of Europeans. One which circulated around Chingola had a large splash of red ink on it to symbolize blood. The other, with YOU HAVE BEEN WARNED! in large white letters on a black background upon its cover, accused Kaunda as near as the laws of libel would allow of violence and extremism. Comments David Mulford:

'The UFP released what in retrospect proved to be the campaign's most devastating propaganda. Particularly damaging was a small UFP brochure entitled "You Have Been Warned", a concise and inflammatory document cleverly designed to summarize Europeans' worst fears, which quoted UNIP's own leaders to drive the points home. The brochure's brutal frankness stunned Northern Rhodesia's complacent Whites and fanned the fears sparked off by the UFP's earlier propaganda.'[1]

It was a nasty campaign, and Morris, by virtue of the fact that UNIP had decided not to oppose him, was firmly nailed to the nationalist party by speaker after speaker on UFP platforms. The battle was between fear and hope, and human nature being what it is, there was little doubt which was the more powerful motivation. Though Morris attracted large audiences before whom he hammered home his conviction of the inevitability of Black rule, and pleaded with Whites to accept gracefully the future, his oratory was wasted, except as a form of entertainment. Down the

[1] D. Mulford, Ibid. p. 283.

road the horrid consequences to Whites and their families of nationalist rule were being painted in lurid colours.

Morris's friends poured superhuman energy into the business of canvassing for support. They plodded round the streets of the town, bearing the brunt of the Whites' long-standing displeasure with the Fighting Parson. They argued and pleaded that the days when Whites could dominate either the country or the Legislature were coming to an end, and that their best protection was in the mutual respect that men like Colin Morris and the Nationalist leaders had for each other.

The Chingola campaign culminated in a flying visit from Sir Roy Welensky, who addressed a packed meeting in the local hotel. The presence of Nchanga Mine's General Manager sporting a huge UFP rosette undoubtedly had its effect. Sir Roy, Great Hero of the Whites, made one of his most effective speeches, skilfully playing upon the basic fears of the Europeans and assuring them that if they reject-ed him they would be defenceless. Welensky's visit was the turning point of the campaign. He succeeded in rallying waverers to the cause and 'converted' a number of voters that Morris's supporters had painfully won round to their way of thinking.

Morris had no Big Name to bring down to speak for him. In an eve-of-poll meeting he tried to repair some of the damage Welensky's speech had done to his campaign. He argued that the inflammatory propaganda being put across by the UFP was destroying any possibility of future trust between the races: 'Even Welensky can't save you from the future,' he declared. 'Even Welensky is not big enough to hold back history.'

It was one of his most effective and prophetic speeches, and he won a great ovation from the crowd, but it was a gesture of appreciation for a game fighter rather than an expression of support. One couple who had attended every one of his meetings expressed to him the dilemma that faced reasonable White voters. 'We know you are right. We can't fault a single one of your arguments, but we have always supported Sir Roy Welensky and we can't let him down now.'

When the votes were counted Magnus had won a decisive victory. The official result read:

Magnus (UFP)   1600

Morris (Ind.)   646

Morris and the Gang retired to one of their houses for a drink, hoarse and exhausted. As they listened to the Election results being broadcast it became clear that Morris had scored more votes than any other non-UFP candidate fighting on the Upper Roll. But it wasn't enough. Still, he never imagined he had six hundred supporters in the whole of Africa, let alone Chingola. Nor did the ex-Liberal Party rebels derive any satisfaction from the news of the obliteration of all the Party's candidates. It was the end of an era. Liberalism, of any political variety, had never been a vigorous growth in Central Africa, and it had proved impotent to survive against the pressures of Nationalist power and European fear.

The Election results immediately confirmed Morris's prediction that African rule was inevitable. The British Government had within a year vindicated his other prophecy that the Federation was doomed by beginning the process of dismantling it. But to be proved right was poor consolation; politics is about the use of power, not the vindication of prophecy.

I I

Colin Morris, unemployed politician, was looking around for a job as a preacher when the Rev. Charles Catto left Chingola for Canada at the end of his tour. The pulpit of Chingola Free Church was vacant. With mock solemnity the Council approached the Rev. Colin Morris to enquire whether he was free to consider an offer. With matching solemnity, the Fighting Parson judiciously considered the offer and then graciously accepted – as though wild horses could have kept him out of that pulpit!

Morris returned to the scene of his old battles, fingered the scarred pulpit Bible, rubbed his hand across the chipped communion table, and reflected on the days of struggle with a certain nostalgia. Things had certainly changed. A failed politician he might be, but he was also a vindicated prophet, accorded a new deference by many who once openly snubbed him. Old animosities might still smoulder, but people were careful to tread delicately. Their old enemy had Friends in High Places!

The old order had passed for ever. Africans walked with a new spring in their step, at long last masters in their own land. Europeans with a bad record in their dealings with Africans packed their bags and stole silently away. The Federation had been hastily unscrambled. Sir Roy Welensky had severed all links with the Territory he had sworn to protect agaist the Black hordes, and took up residence in Salisbury. His portrait came down from public places to be replaced by a smiling Kenneth Kaunda, Prime Minister of Northern Rhodesia and President-Designate of the Independent Republic of Zambia. Whites who had gone fervently to the polls to insure against the Black extremist getting his hands on the reins of power talked fondly of 'our' Prime Minister.

Things had changed in the Church, too. In July 1958, the Copperbelt Free Church Council, representing White Churches, of which Chingola was one, and the Church of Central Africa in Rhodesia which comprised missions in the Northern and Luapula Provinces of the Territory and African congregations on the Copperbelt, united to become the United Church of Central Africa in Rhodesia. Morris's own Church, the Methodist District of Northern Rhodesia, was not a member of this union and carried on its own work in the Southern area of the country, seconding two mini-ters, of whom Morris was one, to the work on the Copper-belt.

Not to put too fine an edge upon it, Morris's negative attitude to all matters of Church administration was widely known and much resented. His only interest in solemn assemblies such as the Methodist Synod was to propose political and social resolutions. When the 'Churchy' business came up, he normally picked up a pal and went to the pictures. Most of the resolutions attacking Federation and demanding African majority rule in Northern Rhod-esia passed by the Methodist Synod between 1958 and 1963 were of his drafting. He confessed to having little faith in these 'paper missiles', but at least they showed that the Church was not taken in by all the guff about Federation, and they helped to mould the thought of the anti-Federation lobbies in Britain. In fairness to his missionary colleagues, it should be stated that these resolutions met little resistance in the Synod. It was Morris's vigorous methods rather than the content of what he said that gave them unease. Apart from the odd missionary who honestly supported Welensky, most of the rest were a-political, not through any lack of courage so much as in loyalty to a conservative tradition of clerical non-intervention in politics.

The head of the United Church of Central Africa in Rhodesia, its President, was elected annually at the Synod. In June, 1963, Colin Morris went along as usual. He made few interventions in the debates, finding 'ecclesiastical plumbing' as uncongenial as ever. He was utterly taken aback when in the vote for the Presidency, his name appeared at the top of the list. The poacher had been made head gamekeeper with a vengeance! The Great Rebel found himself head of a large Church, ultimately responsible for its policy, administration and action. It was doubly significant that he was elected President following an African, the Rev. Jackson Mwape, by a predominantly African Synod, at a time when Africans were displacing Europeans in top jobs in every area of the nation's life. There were those who might shudder with horror at the thought of the Fighting Parson at the head of the Church in the spacious, slow-moving years behind them, but they knew who they needed to steer the Church through the exciting and disturbing days ahead of them. He was 34 years of age.

In a moving ceremony, Morris was invested by the retiring President with the threadbare preaching gown that had once belonged to the great Scottish Nyasaland missionary, Dr Donald Frazer, and had been passed on to the UCCAR by his son George, one of the architects of the Union.

Morris was even more touched the next day to receive a simple, roughly-typed letter headed 'Testimonial to the Rev. Colin Morris, President of the United Church of Central Africa in Rhodesia', and signed by three African ministers on behalf of the rest:

'We, the undersigned, for and on behalf of your African brethren, wish to express our joy on your election to the office of President.

'We give thanks to God for your great leadership of our people over the past seven years. It is only right that you must become head of the Church in the glad year of Independence, for you, more than any other person in the Churches, have led us in the fight for our human dignity. . . . You have a place for sure in the history of our beloved land. . . .'

One compensation for the onerous responsibility of being

'Mr President' was that Morris need not leave Chingola. It was a tradition in the Church that its head should not be a full-time administrator but continue in a pastoral charge. Without doubt, had he been required to leave his pulpit, Morris would have turned the honour down. As it was, there was a mountain of work to be done. The Great Committee-Hater found himself presiding at numerous committees dealing with every aspect of the Church's life from finance to medical work. It involved visits to the Church's stations in the rural areas, and thus many African Christians got their first sight of a man who was a legend to them. His secretary more or less kept him up to the mark with his correspondence, enduring torrents of abuse in the process – 'Becoming President hasn't improved your language!' she snapped after one tirade.

But if the Church had a bear a reluctant administrator, it gained a powerful spokesman. He presented evidence on behalf of the UCCAR to a Commission of Inquiry, chaired by Mr Justice Whelan, into a series of disturbances on the Copperbelt. His analysis of the causes of the trouble sufficiently impressed the Commissioners for them to incorporate it verbatim in their Report.

As Independence Day drew nearer, an event awaited by Africans with intense anticipation and by many Europeans with great nervousness, Morris bent his thoughts towards the problems of Church-State relations that had rocked other parts of Africa. The fruit of his reflection was a fifteen-page Presidential Statement, published in September, 1963 – *Towards a National Church in an Independent Northern Rhodesia*. It was a full-scale analysis of the biblical and theological basis of a Christian's attitude towards the State. After dealing with the question of the nature of Christian protest, a subject on which he had unrivalled authority, he ended by spelling out what the attitude of his Church would be towards the new Zambian State, shortly to come into being:

'The Church should co-operate enthusiastically in the creation of the new State, not devoting its God-given talents solely to "religious" purposes but inextricably involved in the life of the nation at every level. We should avoid perching like vultures upon the shoulders of our new leaders, hoping that they will fail or weakening them by carping criticism. In addition to our historically unchanging tasks we must help to clarify the aims of the State, relating all its policies to the insights of the Gospel. We should not demand for ourselves any pride of place but be content to demonstrate by our life and witness, that we are a salutary influence in our national life. Though we submit ourselves gladly to the authority of our lawful rulers, we must remain ever vigilant, to ensure that the State does not overstep the bounds of its God-given functions, nor use its power in ways that will call down upon it, and us, the Judgement of God.

'It is our prophetic task to draw the attention of the State to the manner of God's dealings with us all. . . .'

The Christians of the United Church of Central Africa in Rhodesia could certainly not claim that they had been given no guidance about their line of duty in the exciting days ahead. Dr Kaunda was delighted with the statement and told his old friend with a grin, 'You keep your half of that bargain, and I'll keep mine!' and added gleefully, 'You'd better behave from now on, Mr President, or I just might deport you!'

At midnight on the 23rd October, 1964, thirty-nine year old Kenneth David Kaunda, poor African minister's son, and Sir Evelyn Hone, Governor of Northern Rhodesia, stood together under the arc lights of the Independence Stadium outside Lusaka. A fanfare from the Trumpeters of the 1st and 2nd Battalions, the Northern Rhodesian Regiment sounded. Then the British National Anthem was played for the last time in a Territory Britain had ruled for forty years. The Union Jack was lowered, a solitary aircraft of the Zambia Air Force flew over the stadium in salute, and then for the first time on an official occasion the new National Anthem of the Republic of Zambia was played, and the green flag of the one-minute-old Republic was raised.

After the military pomp came the religious dedication, and into the spotlight moved three ministers of religion, two African Bishops, the Right Rev. Clement Chabukasanshya of the Roman Catholic Church, and the Right Rev. Filemon Mataka of the Anglican Church. The third was a White man, and a missionary, the President of the United Church of Central Africa in Rhodesia. Whoever had been President of the UCCAR that year would have gained the honour of saying the prayers on this unrepeatable occasion. But it was somehow fitting that it should be the Fighting Parson. Obviously, the President of the new Republic thought it was a good choice too, judging by the broad grin he gave Morris as they passed each other along the red carpet that led to the banks of microphones. Morris bowed gravely as a citizen should to his Head of State, even a state only two minutes old. His voice rang out round the huge stadium: '. . . into Thy hands we commend our land of Zambia. Draw into closer unity the people of all races who dwell here. Deliver us from the pride that fears not God and the selfishness that regards not man, and grant that our new freedom may by Thy blessing be an instrument for good to us and all the nations of the world. . . .'

To commemorate Zambia's independence, President Kaunda established a number of orders and decorations: one, the Order of Freedom, was restricted to those who had served the nation well in the freedom struggle. When the first awards were announced, amongst the names of a handful of Europeans was that of Colin M. Morris, appointed Officer 'for exalted services to the Republic of Zambia'.

Morris, being busy on other things, had taken no part in the negotiations that had led to the creation of the United Church of Central Africa in Rhodesia, but as its President he found himself embroiled in the Union discussions, reaching their final stages, between the UCCAR, the Methodist District of Northern Rhodesia, and the Church of Barotseland, a former mission of the French Reformed Church. Congenial or not, he had to play the part of a church statesman, analysing drafts of Union documents, tinkering with constitutions and having to blow the dust off some of his more weighty theological tomes in order to check a reference here or verify a doctrinal statement there.

Where seven years before he would have argued that the whole wretched business was a waste of time, he had now come to see that the disunity of the Churches in Africa was not only sinful in itself but also destructive of the unity which nationalist leaders were struggling to achieve at nation-building level. At a great missionary meeting in the Liverpool Philharmonic Hall in 1963, Morris said:

'Consider the position in Northern Rhodesia. The Territory is not by any means the most populous, yet there are over seventy tribes represented there, and at a conservative estimate, at least fifty religious organizations, claiming to be Christian. So by simple arithmetic there are, theoretically, one hundred and twenty ways in which the African people can be divided at a time when national unity is the only safeguard against the tribal chaos into which the neighbouring Congo dissolved two years ago. For God's sake, don't let's perpetuate the Methodist and Anglican and Presbyterian tribes as well as the Bemba, Bisa and Lozi. . . .'[1]

Late in 1963, these Union negotiations bogged down, not through any reluctance on the part of the Churches in Africa but because the Methodist Church in Great Britain, the mother-church of the Methodist District, whose permission had to be given for the Union, was dragging its feet. Leading figures in the Union negotiating committee, notably the Rev. Edward G. Nightingale, former Chairman of the Methodist District, felt that a block-buster was required to shake the British Methodist Church out of its torpor on the issue. Since Zambia's own Block-Buster, Colin Morris, was both a minister of the Methodist Church and President of one of the negotiating Churches, he was obviously the man.

[1]C. Morris, *Nothing to Defend*. Cargate Press, 1963, p. 40.

According to Dr Peter Bolink, in his standard work on Church Union in Zambia, Morris flew to London and 'advocated eloquently the issue before the Methodist Annual Conference', pleading the urgent need for unity amongst Christians at a time when Zambia was about to become independent. According to Methodist rules, *two* Annual Conferences had to recommend that an overseas area of the Methodist Church could become autonomous before permission was granted. The Fighting Parson's eloquence had its effect. In the measured words of Bolink ... 'The Conference resolved to depart from its normal procedure and final permission to unite was granted.'[1]

On Saturday, 16th January, 1965, from all parts of the country, delegates, visitors and honoured guests assembled in the Mindolo Church in Kitwe to consummate the creation of the United Church of Zambia from the Methodist District, the UCCAR and the Church of Barotseland. His Excellency, President Kaunda was present and read a lesson. The other lesson was read by Sir Thomas Williams, Speaker of the Zambia Parliament and a keen Methodist who had played a major role in the Union negotiations. At the request of the Church Union Negotiating Committee, Colin Morris preached the sermon. It was a moving, inspiring and historic occasion. As Morris, in his capacity as President of the UCCAR, the Rev. G. Musialela, President of the Church of Barotseland, and the Rev. J. L. Mathews, Chairman of the Methodist Church, signed a copy of the Constitution of the new Church, the dreams were realized of missionaries long gone who, in establishing their tiny missions in remote areas of an empty stretch of Central Africa, prayed for the day when there would be one great Church, an African Church, spanning all their divisions. The largest Protestant Church in Zambia had come into being.

Following the Union Service, a Uniting Synod was held at which officers of the new Church were to be elected. Morris had argued that it was imperative that the President of the new Church should be a Zambian, to signify identi-

[1] P. Bolink, *Towards Church Union in Zambia*. Wever, 1967, pp. 360–361.

fication with the National cause. The delegates of the three former Churches present thought differently. And to Colin Morris fell the honour of being First President of the United Church of Zambia. The Presidential scarf, with Zambian Eagles worked in silver upon it, was placed around his shoulders by another great ecclesiastical controversialist, Lord Soper of Kingsway, who attended the Union ceremony as official representative of the Methodist Church of Great Britain.

The office of President of the United Church of Zambia is subject to annual election. Morris has been re-elected three times. The plethora of committees, multiplied three times since UCCAR days, are a trial, but the ceremonial he loves – Dedicating the Colours of the First Battalion the Zambia Regiment, preaching the Sermon at the National Service on the Anniversary of Independence. In the giddy swirls of changing fortune, the Lancashire working class rebel, the social outcast of the racial struggle, the 'security risk', had become a top Establishment figure.

Yet he was given a sharp reminder of the old days a month after his election to the Presidency of the Church, when a letter from the British High Commissioner in Pretoria, South Africa, informed him that he was no longer permitted to enter that country except with the personal permission of the Minister of the Interior. 'Thank God *someone* still thinks I'm dangerous,' he commented.

There were still perils in his job. A weird Fate had not yet done with Colin Morris, as a headline in the *Times of Zambia* in March, 1965 demonstrates:

LENSHINA ASKS TO JOIN HER OLD CHURCH

Thus began the last episode in the strange confrontation between the Parson and the Prophetess, to steal the headline of a *Guardian* article by Clyde Sanger. But to tell the story properly, of the chaos and murder and violence engendered by a religious woman in the northern areas of Zambia on the eve of Independence, it is necessary to back-track a little.

12

ALICE LENSHINA MULENGA is a religious pheno-
menon, a self-styled prophetess – a simple, illiterate village
woman who had forty thousand fanatical followers prepared
to believe her claim that she died, met and was blessed by
Jesus, rose again from the dead, and began a crusade to
stamp out *buloshi* – witchcraft. This was no harmless religious crankery in an exotic setting. Before the story of
Lenshina had run its course 720 Zambians lay dead, hundreds more were injured, thousands lost their villages and
were cast adrift as refugees – a whole Province of Zambia was devastated in that summer prior to Independence.

Lenshina's Lumpa Church became the cult that 'lost its
head', embroiled Kaunda and his new State, Morris and
the United Church, and led to a bloody confrontation in
which the followers of the prophetess, men, women, and
children, armed only with spears, sticks and pieces of paper
called 'Passports to Heaven', charged fearlessly into mach-
ine gun fire, trusting solely, and futilely, on Alice's promise
that she would turn the soldiers' bullets into water.

The Lumpa uprising is an episode in Zambia's history
everyone would rather forget, except those champions of
White minority governments in Africa who quote it endlessly and inaccurately to demonstrate the unfitness of
Africans to rule themselves. In every sense, those bloody
few weeks scream the failure of Christian missions, of
Government, of the provincial administration, and to those
who witnessed the carnage, the failure of civilization itself.

Let an old African minister, the Rev. Paul Mushindo, who
had dealings with the Lubwa village woman from the be-

ginning, tell the story of the birth of this sect in his own words:

'It was on 18th September, 1953. Alice Lenshina Mulenga Lubusha of Kasomo Village, Chief Nkula's area, gave birth to a child, and became fainted, which shows immorality according to Bemba custom.

'The news went abroad that she was dead. In three days time she rose up again. This untrue rumour attracted many people to her. For about two to five days Alice was being treated for her fainting by people who know the African medicine for such occasions. Then she came to Lubwa to look to the Rev. Paul Mushindo for advice as to how to rejoin the United Church of Central Africa in Rhodesia.

'On 22nd November, 1953, Alice was baptised by the Rev. Mushindo. Now being a full church member she had the right to hold church services. But being an illiterate woman she preached what she had been taught in the catechumen class, the word of God, *but with it* she emphasized that she rose up from the dead; and God has sent her to save people from their sins. This attracted many people to her. Early in 1954, people in the whole district were flowing in like water in coming to her daily. Then in her preachings she used their superstitions. She emphatically said that God had sent her to save people from dying the death caused by *buloshi*. Nearly the whole Northern Province were attracted by such sermons of Alice, more especially the people of the Chinsali and Lundazi districts. At each service, collection would be received, about £20 to £30.

'Suspended members of the UCCAR went to Alice. All people suspected of witchcraft ran away to hide in her protection. By this time some UNIP leaders favoured her. Then she broke away from the UCCAR, and chiefs were forcing their people to join the Alice Lenshina Church. The educated advised her to call her church LUMPA – which means supreme church of the whole world. . . .'

Alice's movement rapidly multiplied, and of the power

of her preaching against witchcraft there can be no argument. In village after village where she spoke, people piled high their bones, powders, beads, and fetish carvings for burning. As a senior missionary of the Church of Scotland who had worked in that area for years commented, 'Alice did more to stamp out witchcraft in five years than the Church succeeded in doing in half a century!' As her fame grew, so did her appetite for power and money. Her supporters built her an imposing 'cathedral' in the village of Sione. A massive structure, put up without White help or missionary funds, it is a monument to what the African people *can* do if really gripped by a cause. Today, as it stands, a ruin with bloodstains on the floor and bullet holes in the door, it is also a monument to what happens when religion gets out of hand and goes crazy.

The Lumpa movement became a weird mixture of good and evil. On the one hand Alice claimed for herself some kind of divine rank, writing a hymn or anthem which was to be sung at all services and gatherings of Lumpa, which proclaimed 'I am the Chief of Chiefs', and predicting that when the day of Independence came, all 'foreign' Churches would be destroyed and only Lumpa would be the Church of the people. On the other hand, in her fight against witchcraft, she did much good, and the strict, if a little puritanical, rules which she enjoined on her members were certainly helpful both to them and the society. One copy of these rules includes the following:

3. Every Christian must not be in the following habits: (a) Backbiting, (b) Insult, (c) Lies, (d) Pride, (e) Boasting, (f) Hatred, (g) Anger, (h) Harsh, (i) False witness, (j) Selfishness (k) Rudeness, (l) Cunning, (m) Stealing etc.

4. Every Christian must keep away from the following: Coveting, Witchcraft, Stealing, Adultery, Sorcery, Witches, Drunkenness, Bad songs and primitive dances.[1]

Paul Mushindo takes up the story again:

'In 1956, Alice Lenshina disobeyed the Native Author-

[1]Taylor & Lehmann. *Christians of the Copperbelt*. S.C.M. Press, 1961, p. 253.

ity and fought against it. Many people were hurt. Alice was not punished by the Central Government so she became worse. At the first elections Alice opposed UNIP and favoured the UFP and visited all her people in the Province as though she had the government in her hand. In 1960, Alice visited the line of rail and it is rumoured that she went to Southern Rhodesia where the Federal Government gave her money. Then in 1961, she came back and held public meetings when nobody with a UNIP card could have membership in her Church. Things began to go wrong, but the Government did not take any notice.

'In 1962, she went to Bright's Village and commanded her attendants to hurt and wound people who refuse to attend her prayers, and wounded men were brought to Lubwa Hospital (UCCAR Mission) to be treated for their wounds by policemen. She was taken off to the Hight Court, but came back happy,[1] and told her followers not to fear anybody, the Government would do her no harm. Still the Government did nothing. In 1963, Lumpa members began to build large villages in many districts without permission of the chiefs. It was in July, 1964, that two Europeans were killed by Lumpa people. Then the Government woke up.'[2]

It is clear in retrospect what happened. As Alice's Church grew, so did UNIP, and for a while she and her movement were almost regarded as a kind of spiritual arm of nationalism, owing nothing to White and missionary influence. Then the masterful Alice, shrewd in matters of religion, made a fatal political error. Jealous of the hold UNIP had upon the people of the Northern Province, Alice decided to change her allegiance and told her people to support the African National Congress. There are certain areas of Zambia, notably the South, where such a decision, though disruptive, would not have led to such calamitous

[1]She was acquitted.
[2]Paul Mushindo – document submitted in evidence to Commission of Enquiry into Lumpa Disturbances.

consequences. But not only was the Northern Province a solid UNIP area but the Chinsali area was Kenneth Kaunda's birthplace. Hence, violent clashes were inevitable. It is probably an uncharitable thought that the Northern Rhodesia Government, which was at that time engaged in the attempt to crush UNIP, might have turned something of a blind eye to Alice's excesses since she had the supreme virtue of being violently anti-UNIP and also wielding great influence in the Northern Province. Campaigns of intimidation and counter-intimidation between Lumpa and UNIP followers ensued. Rival villages were raided, Lumpa churches burned, UNIP followers assaulted. Kaunda, whilst still only leader of UNIP, made a number of attempts to achieve reconcilation with Alice. Sometimes she would not even see him, let alone discuss their differences. Hence a nasty small-scale skirmishing war went on in the Northern Province, obscured from public view by the momentous political happenings centred on the capital, Lusaka.

In 1963, when Alice defied the authority of the local chiefs and began to build her own villages, her motives were possibly two-fold. One was that the harder her people were persecuted the greater became their sense of being the Elect of God, who should draw apart from other people and live in their own way. The other reason is probably that fortified villages of Lumpa were a better protection from the depredations of raiding non-Lumpa than isolated houses in general villages. Whatever the reasons, the drama of Lenshina was approaching its climax.

Late in July 1964, a police Land-Rover went into a Lumpa village to arrest two Lumpas who had assaulted a UNIP member, who had in turn smacked a Lumpa boy. The issue was trivial; the offence probably worth a couple of pounds fine. But it was the detonator that sparked off an explosion of death and hate. The two White policemen were set upon by the villagers, murdered and mutilated beyond description. A detachment of the Police Mobile Unit, who were sent to recover the bodies and arrest the murderers, found themselves facing a vast mob of demented Lumpa follower. They were forced to withdraw – a minor incident had reached the proportions where the army would be required to deal with it.

It was a hopeless battle from the beginning, but such was Alice's hold over her followers that they were utterly convinced that provided they had that little piece of paper in their hands – a 'Passport to Heaven', blessed by Alice – they were immune from death. The Lumpa asked no quarter from the soldiers, and were accorded none. When an army unit approached one of the stockaded Lumpa villages, a Bemba-speaking District Officer, John Hanna, afterwards a close friend of Morris, would appeal through a loud hailer to the villagers to allow the troops and police in quietly – the innocent would not be harmed. There would be a pause followed by the sound of hymn-singing from inside the stockade, then the unearthly roar would grow, showers of stones and blasts from ancient shotguns, which though primitive, were lethal, would herald the opening of the gates, and the whole village, men, women and children, screaming war cries, would charge out brandishing spears and sticks. Shots would be fired over their heads in warning, but it was a waste of ammunition – the mob had left reason or caution far behind. Then the soldiers, many of them new to battle, had to get down to the business of trying to wound moving targets – mothers who charged holding their babies in front of them as shields, men who sheltered behind their womenfolk. Though troops were under strict orders to limit their fire-power to the minimum necessary to stop these suicidal charges, shocked soldiers observing a maniacal Lumpa bearing down upon them with a poised spear could be excused for stopping him any way they could.

This is why many Lumpa died. Many were not content to lie wounded. With legs shattered, arms hanging on by threads of sinew and muscle, they would drag themselves forward, intent only to kill and so inherit the place in heaven promised to them by Alice, who had disappeared into the blue before the shooting started.

What began in 1953 as an isolated case of what might be termed religious mania reached its climax in 1964 in a national emergency.

Colin Morris had been in Sheffield attending the Methodist Conference when the first reports of the trouble were carried in the British Press. He cut short his trip and caught the first available aircraft back to Zambia. Though he had no idea at the time of the magnitude of the trouble, it was in one of his main church mission areas and he felt he ought to be on the spot in case the staff at Lubwa Mission needed reinforcement or the transfer of doctors from mission hospitals elsewhere became necessary.

On his way through Lusaka he called on a very worried Dr Kaunda who, being both gentle by nature and a pacifist by conviction, was utterly appalled by the kind of decision he would have to make in sending up army reinforcements. Less than three months before his country moved serenely and happily into the era of Independence, he found a civil war on his hands and one bedevilled by all kinds of religious implications. At the Prime Minister's suggestion, Morris flew up to the troubled area the next day in an Air Force Dakota. Chinsali *boma*, normally sleeping peacefully in the sun, was the scene of frantic activity. Armed police and soldiers were everywhere. The barbed wire was going up around the detention camp in which Lumpa were to be screened when captured. The little hospital was bursting at the seams with wounded.

Morris talked with police, army, and government officials on the spot. The story was everywhere the same. As soon as a police or army detachment drove up to a fortified Lumpa village, they would be greeted with a fusillade of stones and shotgun pellets followed by a suicidal charge. 'What would happen,' mused Morris aloud, 'if instead of the army approaching these villages, a missionary or African minister fluent in Bemba were to try to get in and reason with the people?' A Senior Police Officer drew his finger across his throat meaningfully. But if the Lumpa would not talk to either the police or the Government, who did that leave but the Church?

The Prime Minister was acutely unhappy at the thought of unarmed churchmen wandering into the middle of a shooting war. But he yielded to Morris's persistence and agreed that unarmed and unescorted reconcilation teams of UCCAR ministers, led by Morris himself, should be given facilities on military aircraft to get to this inaccessible part of the country and do what they could to help bring the fighting to a halt.

Back on the Copperbelt, Morris called a meeting of the staff of the UCCAR. He was looking for ministers, missionaries, and women workers with any knowledge of the Bemba language who were prepared to go into an unpredictable situation. He warned them of the risks and made it clear that anyone who felt unable to go could in no sense be blamed or chided for cowardice. Every single person in the room volunteered. Assigning a skeleton staff to look after the Copperbelt churches, the rest prepared for departure. The Anglican Archbishop, Oliver Green-Wilkinson, in a generous gesture of support offered two Bemba-speaking priests to the team, and the Methodists not only provided a team of ministers but also, through the prompt action of Len Mathews, their General Superintendent, sent off for Methodist relief funds to help pay for the operation. The Secretary of the Christian Council, Edward Nightingale, cabled Geneva for World Council of Churches' Emergency Funds.

A few days later, a British newspaper printed this report from its correspondent in Chinsali:

'I was sitting with a group of newspapermen in the police mess at Chinsali, centre of Northern Rhodesia's strife-torn Northern Province, when a late-night bulletin over the radio announced that the Rev. Colin Morris, President of the United Church of Central Africa in Rhodesia, was flying to Chinsali in an attempt to persuade the followers of Alice Lenshina to return peacefully to their old villages, and to help rehabilitate them. The announcer's voice was drowned by the jeers of police and reporters who had seen the ferocity of the Lumpa warriors at close quarters and had witnessed the frightful atrocities committed on Lumpa villagers by vengeful tribesmen. 'Jesus!' breathed one tired and tipsy police officer, 'Now we're going to have a bunch of bloody parsons saying prayers all over us!' Yet a few days later the jeers had turned to whistles of admiration as Colin Morris and his team moved through bush through which no one would venture without heavy military escort, looking for wounded Lumpa, trying to persuade desperate armed bands of Alice's followers to give themselves up.'

The party flew into Chinsali in Air Force Dakotas, at first twenty-four ministers, missionaries and women workers, later expanded to thirty-five. They carried nothing more lethal than clerical collars and Bemba Testaments. They established their base at Lubwa Mission, birthplace of Kenneth Kaunda and a UCCAR station first established by his father, the Rev. David Kaunda. Lubwa is six miles from Chinsali, the *boma*, and a mere three miles from Sione, cathedral village of Alice Lenshina. The missionary in charge, a robust Church of Scotland missionary, William McKenzie, as brave as a lion, with a somewhat dour exterior that would not change if the Pope dropped in on him for afternoon tea, somehow organized sleeping accommodation for them.

Morris divided the team into three parts. Two ministers and two women workers moved into the vast barbed-wire cages at Chinsali where Lumpa captured in military operations were awaiting either trial or release. They moved amongst them, trying to calm their fears, sort out their family problems, and make representation to the military authorities in cases of undue hardship. They gathered something of the magnitude of their task when small children of five or six would come to them and claim proudly, 'I am Lumpa!'

A second team of three African ministers, a Canadian

missionary and a Canadian woman worker were based sixty miles away at the White Father's mission station at Mulanga where more than three thousand people, fleeing their villages for fear of marauding Lumpa, had collected. Most of them were without food, clothing or blankets. To make matters worse, epidemics of small pox and pneumonia had broken out. Denominational differences forgotten, the team worked alongside the magnificent White Fathers, calming panic, doing necessary first aid, trying to identify orphans, and comforting widows who had lost their men.

Morris and McKenzie led the third team on what the *Methodist Recorder* understated as 'the most unpredictable part of the operation' – visiting villages with which all contact had been lost since the trouble started. McKenzie knew his fifteen thousand square mile parish like the back of his hand. The team travelled, unescorted, along bush paths through country which security forces claimed was swarming with Lumpa gangs. When they made contact with a village, Lumpa or otherwise, they politely asked permission to enter, and if it was granted, they would talk with the village elders, and if it were agreeable, leave behind one of the team to stay with the people and help them to overcome their fears. Then Morris and McKenzie would move on to the next village.

By any standards, this team of churchmen were heroes of the modern Church. Men like William Hincks, Harold Cave, and Tom Gilchrist, all fluent Bemba speakers, helped to damp down panic by their imperturbability, sometimes sleeping alone in a deserted village from which the villagers had fled as night fell for fear of being butchered in the darkness.

Occasionally, on their travels through the bush, Morris and McKenzie were able to report that a Lumpa village had taken down its stockade, one place at least where a bloody confrontation would be unnecessary. Yet on one occasion they entered a Lumpa village where the inhabitants refused to greet them or talk with them; neither did they harm them. But two days later, an army unit arriving at the gates of the same village was met by a homicidal mob. The Providence of God? Protection of clerical collars? Sheer brazen cheek? It depends on your viewpoint and your philosophy of life, but by the law of averages it is little less than a miracle that none of Morris's team were killed. Morris, in fact, sustained the only minor injury, when he had to run a Land-Rover off the road to avoid an army truck whose brakes had failed. A nasty gash in his scalp, but he was soon on his way again. Answering a press reporter's provocative question whether he had acted irresponsibly in taking unarmed missionaries and ministers into a war situation, Morris replied: 'Every member of the team was a volunteer who knew precisely what he or she was facing. Furthermore, I don't think the risks were greater than those which the early missionaries faced when they first encountered untamed Africa. It seems to me that even in 1964, danger is an occupational hazard of the missionary which he's got to face up to. Anyone who comes out to Africa as a missionary must recognize that this is a continent in ferment. He could get hurt. . . .'

If courage was one requirement for the team, a strong stomach was the other. Sometimes they would have to stop on their journeyings in order to bury a dead Lumpa who had crawled away wounded into the bush. Or to get help to wounded Lumpa who had been shot and whose wounds had been festering for weeks. To one of the team there fell the dreadful task of helping to dig the communal grave for the inhabitants of a small village who had been surprised by Lumpa, mutilated and massacred.

The surrender of Alice Lenshina to the Government took much of the steam out of the fighting. Then began the serious work of reconcilation as the Lumpa villages were destroyed and their inhabitants were taken back to their former homes. How would the villagers receive them? The answer, said Morris, is the village Christian. It is his his duty to welcome back these pathetic people. And in many cases they did. Morris's team would take a Lumpa family back to its original village and confer with the elders, whilst the family sat dumbly in the back of the Land-Rover and awaited their fate. Then a group of village Christians would emerge with gifts of eggs and mealie meal, overwhelming the astonished and fearful Lumpa with kindness. Such scenes made the effort and danger well worthwhile. It says much for these village Christians that they were prepared to forget the bloody past; they would not find it easy to accept as neighbours people who might have been implicated in the death of one of their relatives. Though the Church might well have failed in handling the Lenshina affair when Alice first announced her death and resurrection, it did much to redeem the past by the way ministers and missionaries worked under terrible conditions to achieve reconcilation in the war-torn Northern Province, and by the way Christian villagers offered the hand of friendship to former deadly enemies.

Kenneth Kaunda had little option but to ban the Lumpa Movement. Alice and some of her deacons were placed in restriction at Mumbwa, near Lusaka, for their own safety and in the public interest. The press men flew on to the next trouble spot, never far away in modern Africa, the army packed up their camps and trundled down the Great North Road in trucks. The Zambia Government relieved the Churches of the task of feeding and rehabilitating the Lumpa, aided by generous gifts from the British Red Cross and the Women's Voluntary Service of Zambia.

The Fighting Parson's team returned to their routine work, exhausted yet exhilarated. For once the Church had really been on the spot when most needed and in a position to offer what was urgently required – the gift of reconciliation. The Secretary of the Christian Council, Edward G. Nightingale, in a letter to the World Council of Churches, wrote, 'It has been the most dramatic demonstration of the Christian Church in action that I have seen in a pretty long experience of Church work in Africa. . . .'

Yet over the whole Northern Province remained a gigantic question mark – who or what would fill the vacuum left by the banning of the Lumpa? For the two Churches traditionally involved in the work of the area, the Catholics and the UCCAR, there was much heart-searching and policy planning. For whatever Alice Lenshina Mulenga had given the people of that area, it had been powerful enough to destroy witchcraft, and strong enough to have them charging to certain death, singing. A dead-tired President of the UCCAR had much to think about as he returned to Chingola.

Because much propaganda has been made against the Republic of Zambia as a consequence of the Lumpa war it is only fair to reproduce a transcript of a press interview given by Colin Morris at Chinsali at the end of the Church operation, and printed in many newspapers. The questions asked had come into the minds of thousands reading of those terrible weeks or watching appalling scenes on the world's television networks. One reporter put them for everyone:

Q. A certain section of the overseas press has taken the line that the military operations against the Lumpa were a systematic attempt by Government to destroy the religious freedom of a harmless sect. Is there any truth in this?

A. I would say that this interpretation is unmitigated nonsense. The Lumpa leaders who incited their people to violence were not fighting for religious freedom. They already had it. They were fighting for the right to remain above the law; the right to establish a private state within the State, and the right to offer violence with impunity to the representatives of law and order. No government could ignore a challenge of this kind without forfeiting the right to rule.

Q. But is it not true that certain elements in UNIP have been guilty of intimidating the Lumpa people for their refusal to carry party cards?

A. Yes, it is true that UNIP have been guilty of intimidation against the Lumpa people. But I don't think that this is the fact upon which all else hinges. In the first place, no amount of intimidation justifies the murder of

140

policemen and innocent villagers. In the second place, since Dr Kaunda told his people to leave the Lumpa alone about eighteen months ago, party discipline has been pretty good and in the vast majority of incidents that have occurred, UNIP members have been the victims rather than the aggressors.

There are two sides to this intimidation question. The Lumpa people themselves went in for a fair amount of intimidation, as the members of Christian Churches in the area can testify.

Q. It has been claimed that the ferocity of the Government's reaction was out of all proportion to the trouble the Lumpa were causing. What would you say to this?

A. Let's be clear about this. Armed intervention by Government forces only followed the cold-blooded murder of two policemen going about their lawful occasions. It seems to me that if you offer unprovoked violence to the police and incite hundreds of your followers to attack them, you are setting in train a series of events in which many people are going to get hurt. If there are any grounds for criticism of the Government they would not be that they took unduly severe action but rather that they did not act firmly years ago.

Q. But doesn't the fate of the Lumpa Church make you apprehensive about the freedom of your own or any other Church to pursue its beliefs without interference?

A. Not at all. If my own Church were to set itself up as beyond law, refuse to acknowledge civil authority, and countenance the murder of innocent people, we would deserve all we got.

Q. There have been allegations that undue brutality was used by the police and army in destroying stockaded villages. What is your own view?

A. Only those who were present at every single action could express any opinion worth listening to, on this one. I was not, but what I did see was that occasionally individual soldiers kept on firing after the order to cease fire had been given. But then a charge of crazed warriors is a hair-raising spectacle, and it would not be surprising if odd individuals lost their heads. But all I have been able to discover points to the fact that the army and police used the minimum fire power necessary to neutralize resistance.

Q. Would you call the Lumpas Christians?

A. I don't believe in making mass judgements about people. I suppose the answer is that many Lumpas were and are honest, God-fearing citizens. But I would hesitate to describe as Christians those who incited small children to murder, whose women-folk made spear-attacks holding their babies in front of them as shields, and whose menfolk fought battles hiding behind groups of their children. Would you?

Q. What would you say was the secret of Alice's religious success?

A. Three-fold, I think. Firstly, she appeared on the scene at the psychological moment, politically speaking. The sect came into existence in 1953, the year Federation was imposed upon Northern Rhodesia and many Africans were disillusioned with the Churches because they felt that a strong enough fight had not been put up by them against Federation. Therefore, a non-White, totally African religion suited the mood of the moment.

Secondly, the nub of Alice's preaching at the outset was an attack upon witchcraft. I think it is true that she freed thousands of villagers from their fear of witchcraft by offering them a power to overcome it. Here, I think the Churches failed because, too often, they refused to face up to the hold which witchcraft had upon many villagers. They dismissed it as a delusion and, therefore, could offer no defence against it.

Thirdly, Lenshina is, in some sense, a person with a genius for religion. She composed hymns and songs set to traditional African music, and expressing a genuine African cast of thought. The people had no sense that the faith she held or preached was a foreign importation. We failed them badly there, I think.

But the Fighting Parson's dealing with the Militant Prophetess was not yet over. On a wet day in March 1965, the President of the United Church of Zambia received a letter from a prominent firm of lawyers acting for Alice in the matter of a Tribunal which had been convened to determine whether she should remain in detention. The letter said '. . . our client has instructed us that she wishes to do everything possible to heal the schism between the United Church of Zambia and her followers, and in order to achieve this she has asked us to approach you, with a view to your arranging an interview with a representative of the UCZ, particularly if possible the Reverend Paul Mushindo. . . .'

Morris had faced tricky problems throughout his ministry in Africa, but this was undoubtedly the knottiest. In fairness to the Government of Zambia, who were still trying to clear up the mess in the Lumpa areas, he felt he should consult Dr Kaunda on the matter. This compassionate man, who above all things wants the people in his land to live in harmony together, agreed to provide facilities for whoever Morris nominated to see Alice privately at the detention centre in Mumbwa. Both knew that Alice's reconcilation with her former Church was the only hope of a permanent solution to the problem she presented, and both knew the chances were slim but worth taking.

The three-man team which Morris appointed to interview Alice consisted of the Rev. Paul Mushindo, the old minister who had baptized her before she broke away from the Church, the Rev. Fergus MacPherson, a former Church of Scotland missionary who was stationed at Lubwa, and the Rev. Doyce Musunsa, Clerk of Synod of the United Church of Zambia. Morris decided not to see her himself at that stage, partly because he felt she would be more comfortable with men she knew from the old days, and partly because he had not the grasp of the Bemba language necessary to converse with her except through an interpreter, which he thought would be inhibiting. He was also grateful that she trusted him sufficiently in spite of his long-standing association with her arch-enemy Dr Kaunda, to request through her lawyers that Morris should be a member of the Commission of Inquiry to be appointed to investigate the Lumpa troubles – though his membership was out of the question since he had been too closely involved in the events under review.

The three-man team found themselves with a very resentful Alice on their hands when they met her at Mumbwa. The previous week a Tribunal had met to consider whether or not her continued detention was justified, and she had taken exception to the perfectly reasonable argument from the Attorney-General that her release before the total picture in the Chinsali area was clearer might result in a new flare-up of violence. Commented one of the team, 'her remarks were made with great fluency, but full of self-centred resentment. But she showed interest in our first hand report of people and places in Chinsali . . . she cried a little and protested that she had nothing to teach anybody and nothing to say.' But she agreed to meet the team again.

At the second meeting, Alice denied all responsibility for the deaths during the Lumpa war, blaming the whole thing on the Government. She remained truculent and resentful. But a breakthrough came at the third session when the delegates detected some sign that she wished to speak to them alone rather than surrounded by her deacons. She also seemed more willing to listen to reason. In the fourth meeting, Alice remarked that she wanted to leave Zambia 'where there is no peace for me'. She would like to go to Malawi, Uganda, or Kenya. She reiterated that she had no further interest in the Lumpa movement. She made a gift of it to the delegation, and said that her only concern was that her followers rejoin their original Churches. She showed neither interest nor concern in the plight of her people starving in the bush, which, she insisted, was not her fault.

Alice also claimed that spiritual power had left her, and that all she wanted to do was live a normal life, preferably outside Zambia. By this time the team had formed a strong impression that she was spiritually disorientated. Whatever the mysterious power was that had taken hold on her, it had gone just as inexplicably. She was once more the simple village woman – except that she dominated those of her deacons who were with her to such an extent that it gave the lie to any suggestion that she had been a mere figure-head, just a tool in the hands of unscrupulous men. With or without the power, Alice was boss. The team reported their findings to Morris who meanwhile had been puzzling out some kind of formula for receiving her back into the United Church of Zambia. It was, he commented to a *Guardian* correspondent, '. . . like carrying on an *Honest to God* debate on the slopes of a rumbling volcano!'

Tremendous press and public interest was aroused when Alice's lawyers made public her request for reconcilation with the United Church of Zambia, and in some areas, particularly around Lubwa, African Christians were darkly suspicious that some kind of undercover deal might be done with the Prophetess, who, to their mind, had caused such suffering to them and the Church. Bill MacKenzie and Paul Mushindo, who had gone on with the business of picking up the pieces in the Chinsali area when Morris's team withdrew, warned him that some of the chiefs and people had misunderstood the press reports they had heard about Alice's request, and thought that the UCZ intended to bring Alice back to the Lubwa Church as some kind of leader. 'We shall know how to deal with her if she sets foot in this place,' these outraged villagers said darkly. On the other hand, Morris knew that reconciliation between the UCZ and Alice would be meaningless unless it took place finally where the Lenshina movement began – from Lubwa Church.

Anxious that dangerous misunderstandings should not get around the Church and country because of the press interest in the strange spectacle of the Parson and Prophetess beginning a theological courtship, Morris decided to publish a document setting out a possible formula for restoring Alice to membership of his Church. It was, he emphasised,

solely a basis for discussion, and not an official pronounce-
ment. As the *Guardian* correspondent wrote, 'To avoid the
courts of the UCZ becoming the scene of a spectacular
heresy trial Morris has assumed personal responsibility for
the negotiations with Alice in the hope that continuous
dialogue may produce a compromise which has a fighting
chance of acceptance by both sides.'

Morris's particular problem was Alice's claim to have
risen from the dead. The general view amongst his colleagues
was that she must renounce this claim as a delusion. He was
more agnostic. 'We don't know,' he argued, 'and things
just as strange have happened in the history of the Church.
We bellow from our pulpits all these Gospel promises that
faith the size of a grain of mustard seed will shift a mountain,
or that anyone who believes in Jesus, even if he dies will live
again, then the minute someone claims to have done it we
say they're deluded. We . . . don't . . . know!' Some
churchmen felt that Morris's solution to this problem was
more an exercise in verbal ingenuity than an answer. Yet
it is difficult to see what else he could have proposed short
of a demand that she renounce her miraculous claim – a
condition he could not conscientiously lay down, and which
he was sure Alice would not accept since she obviously
sincerely believed what she said about those fantastic five
days in the bush when Jesus raised her from the dead and
gave her a message.

Said Morris's document:

'The Church has no way of adjudicating Alice's claim
to have risen from the dead. Only God knows the whole
truth. In human terms, the important thing is that Alice
sincerely believes that she underwent this experience and
her belief has been attested by the transformation of a
simple village woman into a dynamic religious leader
who, in the early days of her movement, did much good.
The Church has always recognized that God's power
came upon men and women in ways foreign to human
understanding and that in such cases the only thing to be
done was to 'test the spirits to see whether they be of

146

God' by examining the uses to which unusual spiritual power was put by those claiming it. . . . suffice it to say that as a result of whatever experience she underwent, she was given the gift of prophecy and ministry.'

On the question of Alice's involvement in the violent disturbances, Morris's document said that it was the rôle of the State to exact justice and that of the Church to offer forgiveness after due reparation: 'The Church has neither the right nor the authority to constitute itself into a tribunal to judge the legal and political aspects of the Lumpa disturbances. But it must ask a number of important questions:

1. Is there evidence of genuine penitence for the hurt caused through the misuse of spiritual gifts?

2. Does Alice recognize that any prophetic movement cut off from the life and discipline of the historical Church becomes perverted and increasingly destructive of the spiritual and social good?

3. Is Alice aware of the blasphemy of becoming the object of her followers' worship and prepared to rebuke those who make extravagant claims for her in the future?

Confessing that the Church was not without blame for the Lumpa tragedy, the document concluded: 'We would hope that Alice's gifts could be channelled through the Church and that the Church would have the breadth of understanding to accept Alice's service as an expression of genuine indigenous Christianity, always provided that this expression does not conflict with New Testament Faith.'

But the theological problems were only the tip of the iceberg. What on earth could be done with Alice within the United Church of Zambia? It was out of the question that Alice should become an ordinary member of one of the village women's groups, content to knit, sew and sing choruses whilst the menfolk ran the church. She still had a magic name, and would be a drawing card of such magnitude that she would excite the envy of all but the most understanding of African ministers. And when her followers flooded into the Church after her? Once the Lumpa spiritual powerhouse began to hum within the structures of an institutional Church might it not tear them apart and recreate it into an organization whose image was sharply different from a traditionally Christian one? Morris's own view was that the risk was worth taking in order to harness constructively what spiritual dynamism was left in the Lumpa movement, provided that the end result, however foreign to Western missionary patterns, was still recognizably of the New Testament.

The political dimensions of Morris's headache were well summarized by Richard Hall in a *Guardian* article:

'The UCZ has a pro-nationalist image – a priceless asset in an independent African State. This image is largely the result of the identification with the African cause in Federation days of Morris himself and missionaries like Merfyn Temple. Yet in the eyes of many Zambians – even, it is rumoured, of certain Cabinet Ministers – Alice is widely regarded as a traitor who would be escaping her just deserts if she were re-integrated into society through membership of the UCZ, which would probably be accused of un-Zambian activity by receiving her.

'Morris, who has campaigned indefatigably for Christian political involvement in Africa, would find the loss of this favourable image a bitter pill to swallow. . . .'

Hall goes on to speculate about a possibility that Morris has never voiced to *anybody* but which must have occurred to him:

'Niggling, too, at the mind of the President of the UCZ must be the uneasy suspicion, openly voiced in some Government circles, that Alice's appeal for reconciliation was a shrewd tactical move to secure her release, with the possibility that once free she might begin organizing and preaching again, thus taking the country back to the opening move of the game.'

Some unworldly prelate might be excused for not considering the possibility that Alice was 'trying it on', but not Morris, who knew every nuance of the political game and had a reputation, complimentary or otherwise, for being a superb tactician.

Whilst the theologians argued about Morris's document and certain African Christians in the Northern Province muttered their dark suspicions that the one who had disrupted the life of their Church and society might re-appear amongst them in the guise of a penitent, Morris and Doyce Musunsa carried on the talks with Alice in her Mumbwa detention camp. No record actually exists of the first meeting between the Fighting Parson and the Militant Prophetess, but Morris found himself agreeing with the original negotiating team that Alice was so spiritually disorientated that all theological argument about Resurrection from the Dead and the like was out of the question. She needed pastoral help. A senior Zambian minister in the Mumbwa area was given the care of her with strict instructions not to attempt to argue or talk her into anything. The village woman who started a war seemed to have lost her spiritual bearings.

Morris's plan went into the filing cabinet. Alice was moved to Kalabo in Barotse Province where she worships quietly with a UCZ congregation on Sundays. Lumpa's leader seems to have become a 'burnt out case' – possessed by some powerful spirit, used, and then discarded. But if Lumpa as a spiritual movement seems dead, politically it remains a serious problem. Thousands of Lumpas who fled during and after the troubles remain encamped just over the Congo border at Mokambo – an embarrassment equally to both Zambian and Congolese Governments. For this generation at least, Zambia seems to have added another tribe – Lumpa – to the multiplicity of existing ones that President Kaunda is striving to mould into one nation.

But if at some future time, when bitterness has abated, some future President of the United Church of Zambia finds himself confronted with Alice's membership application, duly written out and endorsed by a congregation, he will find a full-scale blue-print with formula and procedure already worked out for him somewhere amongst the papers Morris hands on to him . . . that is, of course, if the Fighting Parson, with his renowned administrative competence, hasn't lost, mislaid or burnt it!

13

SINCE Alice Lenshina Mulenga has disappeared into obscurity, Colin Morris's life has been free of the major crises that were his meat and drink for so long. He runs a busy church – Chingola Free Church has been re-named St Mark's – and as President has responsibility for missions scattered around an area the size of Europe. In order to cope with Zambia's vast distances, he learned to fly in 1966, obtaining a pilot's licence after fifty student-hours bouncing around in the skies above the Central African Plateau. He took to the medium as he does to every new experience, especially if there is an element of risk involved – with a great sense of exhilaration.

Having strenuously advocated African rule in Zambia, Morris has been greatly caught up in post-independence developments. In 1967, President Kaunda appointed him chairman of a Commission to bring together three African trade unions in the copper industry which had been at each other's throats for years with catastrophic consequences for industrial peace. After months of painstaking negotiation, the Mineworkers' Union of Zambia emerged as a monument to his diplomatic skill. His appointment to the Income Tax Appeal Board seemed a wry joke since one of his absolute blind spots is the ability to make sense of even the simplest of calculations; lack of mechanical aptitude is the other. If he so much as mentions that he intends to knock a nail in his study wall to hang a picture, Church Council members blench with horror at the prospect of an expanse of gouged-out plaster and bent nails on Church property, and scurry to help him.

Then there is the world travel which makes him 'Our

Invisible Man at St Mark's' – 'Who's the visiting preacher?' the Church Secretary asked sarcastically of his wife when Morris appeared through the vestry door one recent Sunday to conduct the service. A regular visitor to the United States, he has proved a great success with student audiences who relish the streak of rebelliousness in him, his biting wit, and his record as a freedom fighter. If the volume of invitations from university campuses is any indication, he certainly has the Word for a generation in revolt. Because Zambia is the jumping-off point for revolutionary freedom movements operating in Rhodesia, Angola, and Mozambique, Morris has first hand knowledge of the techniques of armed struggle and has mastered the writings of left-wing theorists such as Fanon, Che Guevara, Ho Chi Minh and Torres – 'They are writing the theology of our time,' he told an enthusiastic gathering of Washington students. Senior churchmen who had invited the 'distinguished missionary' over in the hope that he would be able to channel student anger into more 'constructive' spheres were highly displeased to find him aiding and abetting a rebellion. He was not playing up to his audience. One of the most disconcerting aspects of his thinking is the deep conviction that the West is doomed by its greed, racial discrimination and inability to come to terms with a world in revolution:

The glory of the West is in reality only a magnificent decadence hidden behind a phalanx of gleaming machines which are the last kick of the Renaissance. There is plenty of activity but it is not the disciplined movement of men of purpose. It is the crazy gallop of a chicken with its head cut off. Everything has deserted the West: inspiration, art, even God. For on the basis of their own theology, presumably a God who appears in history can also disappear. They talk about the death of God but it is more likely that He has withdrawn in disgust.'

Sentiments like these set his hearers hotly debating whether he is a modern prophet or a destructive demagogue. How far his views on the inevitability of violent revolution can be reconciled with Christianity is a matter for the theologians to decide, but his passionate advocacy of the cause of the underdog and his attacks upon the three constituencies he calls the Unyoung, Uncoloured and Unpoor, ring more like the Old Testament than the New Theology.

In February 1968, Morris visited Vietnam and, true to form, his arrival coincided with the Tet Offensive when the Vietcong and North Vietnamese launched heavy attacks throughout the entire country. This story almost came to a suitably dramatic end. Whilst flying from the U.S. air base at Bankok to Tan Son Nhut air base, Saigon, the C47 troop carrier in which he was travelling was accidentally hit by a U.S. artillery shell over the Mekong Delta. One wing was extensively damaged. Parachutes were doled out to the passengers, who included a relief aircrew for a giant B52 bomber and a couple of International Red Cross officials. They were given the option of bailing out or risking an emergency landing. Morris, eyeing apprehensively Vietcong country seven thousand feet below, and deciding he would have difficulty in convincing the V.C. that he was a non-combatant if he descended upon them wearing an Air Force parachute, chose to stay with the aircraft, which managed to make a bone-jarring landing at an emergency airstrip. One of the crew took a photograph of a parachute-laden Morris, pipe grimly clenched between teeth, staring fixedly at the damaged wing as though willing it to stay together.

Two of Colin Morris's great ambitions were fulfilled in 1968. One of his old friends, the Rev. Jackson Mwape, was appointed to take his place as President of the United Church of Zambia from January 1969. The entire leadership of a great Church has passed into Zambian hands, a goal for which Morris had worked for years. And on Palm Sunday, 1968, he and five other ministers ordained the first woman to his Church's ministry. Morris's quip at the World Council seven years before about the number of women of both sexes running the modern Church was just that − a verbal quip. He has long been an advocate of opening the ranks of the ministry to women, and the Rev. Peggy Hiscock is the embodiment of one of his deepest convictions that Africa's nationalist awakening must be followed by a second revolution which will release the potential locked up in the continent's subjugated women.

Proof that his crusading zeal had not been blunted by his spell as an ecclesiastical V.I.P. was furnished as a result of an incident which occurred in his own town at the end of 1967. A Zambian dropped dead of hunger just a few hundred yards from his front door. It was a freak happening on the Copperbelt, of all parts of the country, where wages are relatively high and the people prosperous in relation to their rural counterparts. But to him, the hungry little man was a prophetic sign. He dashed off a biting article to the *Methodist Recorder*, addressing a British Methodist Church apparently so obsessed with the niceties of Union negotiation with the Church of England, and pleading to Christians to come to terms with the *real* world, not made up of bishops, vestments and liturgies, but of hunger, discrimination and underprivilege. The article's tone smacks both of indignation and personal guilt. There is no doubt that this incident had a traumatic effect upon Morris, who felt a sense of personal responsibility about his own comparative affluence in the midst of a poor continent.

He followed up the article by developing its theme in a hundred-page book, written at white heat and significantly titled *Include Me Out!*[1] Its theme is simple. The Church is dying because it is a rich Church in a poor world; whilst it tinkers with its structures and perpetuates a fantasy life, a whole starving world cries aloud to God for justice. It is an attack on theologians who are revolutionary at the level of argument rather than action, and upon churchmen for whom the way water if poured over a baby's head at baptism takes priority over crusts held out to starving men. The book is a heart-cry for the Church to rediscover the truth that 'Christianity is humane action for

[1]Epworth Press, 1968.

154

Jesus' sake, at some cost to myself; that, and nothing much else.'

Include Me Out! is Morris at his most scintillating and, some would say, his most unfair. In it can be detected the old tendency to undervalue those less dramatic ministries which doggedly turn the wheel of the grindstone that throws off incandescent sparks like Morris. The argument is drastically over-simplified; complex issues are reduced to stark blacks and whites, and qualifications are brushed aside. There is the sharp, almost bitter polemic of the platform virtuoso:

'Obscenity is the jewelled ring on a bishop's finger. It is the flash of the gold wrist watch from under the sleeve of my cassock as I throw dirt on the coffin of a man who died of starvation, murmuring the while, the most asinine words in the English language – "Since it pleased Almighty God to take to himself our brother." Obscenity is the cardinal who cries "Murder!" when a woman aborts a piece of bloody tissue, but keeps silent or indeed gives his blessing whilst thousands of fully formed sons and daughters of women are incinerated in Viet Nam. . . .

Obscenity is the scurryings hither and thither of us homberg-hatted clerics with our bulging brief cases and our crowded diaries, protesting that the reasons for our frenzied activity is the desire to be Christ to that little man with the shrunken stomach.'[1]

Here, too, is to be detected the love-hate relationship Morris has had with the Church for so long:

'Though I would like to call myself a true rebel, I cannot cut myself free from the Church. This is not only because I have a personal share of responsibility for her failures and so must stand the racket, but also because it was through the cracked and distorting mirror of the Church that I first saw the One by whose side I seek to take my stand in the life of the world.'

One would miss the whole point of the Morris theology

[1] *Op. Cit.* p. 43.

by putting the argument of *Include Me Out!* under a microscope and recording the inconsistencies. It is a pamphlet in the tradition of Dean Jonathan Swift rather than a work of theological reconstruction in the genre of Bishop John Robinson. It is meant to deliver a blow to the belly rather than provoke a scratching of the head. The *New Christian*, in its review, described the book as 'the most significant since *Honest to God!*' and the Bishop of Woolwich wrote of it as 'splendid and searing stuff'. More conservative journals were not so enthusiastic. All agreed that it was a brilliant piece of polemical writing but felt that Christian theology had been so brutally hacked about as to raise questions whether Morris was a Christian at all.

Include Me Out! certainly touched a raw nerve in the Church. It went through seven editions in the first six months from publication, selling twenty-five thousand copies. Morris, hitherto known mainly to students of the African scene, and in Methodist circles, became a household name (and not necessarily a flattering one) throughout the Church. He had stirred Christians with the hot blast of a kind of truth which cut through layers of institutional irrelevancy and, by the response gained, proved that there is still a caring heart beating within a Church which many dismissed as a decaying corpse. The book does not tell the whole story, but it tells a story that had to be told, and tells it magnificently.

The news that Colin Morris was to lay down the leadership of the United Church of Zambia prompted much conjecture in ecclesiastical circles as to the shape of his future. Speculation gave way to mystification in April 1968, when the *Methodist Recorder* reported: 'The Rev. Colin M. Morris, President of the United Church of Zambia, has provisionally accepted an invitation to become Minister of Wesley's Chapel, London, from September, 1969.'

The *Guardian's* 'Miscellany' column, in a comment on the appointment, quoted an unnamed 'senior Methodist' as exclaiming on hearing the news, The mind boggles! What happens when you put a volcano down in a graveyard?

'Wesley's Chapel, City Road, London has been described as the Cathedral Church of Methodism. As Mother Church of a world-wide family and the seat and shrine of its only real bishopric, the title is not inappropriate.'[1] Thus writes the Chapel's historian. Built by John Wesley himself, whose house, preserved as a national monument, is on the site, and who is buried with many other distinguished early Methodists in the grounds, Wesley's Chapel is a beautiful, traditional structure, widely revered but sparsely attended because it stands in the commercial sector of the City of London, which is as deserted as a tomb over the week-end. This magnificent marble and mahogany structure, whose atmosphere breathes traditionalism and respect for the past, is the last place that many churchmen could see the Fighting Parson settling into, adapting himself to a gracious, measured pace of life. Argument has raged both about the wisdom of offering him the job and his wisdom in accepting it. Officially, Morris has said nothing other than in an untypically brief press statement when he announced, 'I have been honoured by the invitation to become Minister of Wesley's Chapel, London. I have accepted this call. I leave Africa with great regret.' He has made no other comment, and clearly does not intend to do so, though he cannot be without inner uncertainty about the rightness of such a drastic change of environment. Many Methodist eyes are bound to turn towards City Road in September 1969, to see what the incorrigible rebel does with the international shrine.

The reasons why Morris is leaving Africa's sunny skies at all for the dark caverns of the City of London are somewhat easier to conjecture because he has written much on the expendability of the missionary. Having led for so long the United Church of Zambia, he clearly does not intend to linger on in order to cast a shadow over his Zambian successor. Not for him the role of the White eminence behind the Black throne. The break is to be a clean one – 'New leadership for a new day!' was the theme of his final

[1]Max W. Woodward, *One At London*. Epworth Press, 1966, p. 13.

address to the Church's Synod, at which his successor was invested. He is acutely conscious that newly emancipated Africans do not wish to be reminded of their one-time dependency upon people like himself as they face up to the gigantic challenge of ensuring the survival of their nations. The work which he was peculiarly equipped to do is over – the blasting job complete, the more dramatic aspects of the battle finished. There *will* be missionaries in the ranks of the African-led Church, but they will be a generation of men who accept independence as a fact of life, who have never known a state of affairs where Africans did not rule their own country. These new men, probably less tempestuous than the likes of Morris and his comrade Merfyn Temple, will demonstrate the non-racial nature of the Church in Africa, and help carry the revolution through to its next stage.

Politically, too, Colin Morris, who ponders long over the thorny problem of the White minority regimes in Southern Africa, senses that the centre of gravity of that struggle has shifted from the African Continent to the world centres of power where the vigorous lobbying must take place to prevent a sell-out of the African peoples. Wherever his future takes him, he will turn his surroundings into a front line from which to fight the cause of his beloved Africa.